Living Lives in Quiet Desperation

...the pain of homelessness

Living Lives in Quiet Desperation

...the pain of homelessness

Dr. Marilyn Reitz-Pustejovsky

PALMETTO
P U B L I S H I N G
Charleston, SC
www.PalmettoPublishing.com

Paperback ISBN: 9798822968684
eBook ISBN: 9798822968691

"We think sometimes that poverty is only being hungry, naked and homeless. The poverty of being unwanted, unloved and uncared for is the real test of poverty"

Mother Theresa

Dedication

This book is dedicated to the thousands of men, women and children for whom I have deep compassion. The slow slide to living without a domicile on the street, produces fear and hopelessness. If they have no family or friends to help them, they are caught in an untenable situation. If nothing changes, there are no answers and no solutions. They have no choice but to live their lives in quiet desperation.

Dr. Marilyn Reitz-Pustejovsky

About the Author

Dr. Marilyn Reitz-Pustejovsky has received four college degrees from the University of Houston, University Park, Houston, Texas. She has two undergraduate degrees, in psychology, and sociology, a master's degree in social work, and a doctorate in educational psychology.

Marilyn has been published in the *Journal for Social Distress and the Homeless*. She has written and published two books for first graders: *Joey, Having A Hurting Heart* in English, and translated it into Spanish. She wrote her dissertation on the homeless but never published it. Twenty years later at age 79, she saw how devastated the people living homeless were in the COVID-19 pandemic. She wanted to draw attention to how hard the lives of the homeless were and decided to use her previous research and write a publishable graduate-level book.

Marilyn lives in Bellaire, Texas with her daughter and another homeless shelter dog, Cookie. Dixie is the beautiful Labrador in this picture. Dixie died of cancer two years after being rescued from the animal shelter.

TABLE OF CONTENTS

INTRODUCTION

The best way to introduce the subject of my book is to tell you a true story. This little boy was about four years old. His parents died of substance abuse and homelessness. Jacob went to live with a great aunt. She punished him by locking him in the room under the stairs. When he was 13, he ran away. He joined some homeless people. He ended up staying in the same area with the same people until they died. He learned how to survive. He did not talk much. He just learned to exist. He lived a sad, quiet life. During the COVID-19 pandemic, he had no place to stay because the police had raided the tent city where he lived. Everything was destroyed. He died of COVID-19.

The poor and homeless have existed throughout history but not until the modern era has homelessness been considered a social and an economic problem (Geremek, 1994; Anderson, et al., 1998; Spence, 1985). In the last two decades of the twentieth century, researchers have found that more than seven million Americans have experienced homelessness at least once in their lives (Burt, 1989; Sullivan et al., 2000). While there are many causes, persistent poverty has been the decisive factor turning temporary crises into extended periods of homelessness. Society's current response to homelessness is to offer care through relief efforts that are focused on temporary solutions for emergency management (Pustejovsky, 2002)

Twenty years after the original collection of this data documenting the state of the people living homeless (at that time), some things have changed while the plight of people living homeless is still critical. The COVID-19 pandemic appeared highlighting many conditions and attitudes that have remained disturbingly the same. The existing welfare state, having been set up to manage people affected by lack of shelter, medical services, and food services, was devastated by the pandemic. While the paradigm has altered, it has not shifted enough to expose real solutions. Men women and children living homeless remained exposed to the same lack of meaningful differences in their lives. The people living without domiciles have remained, for the most part, disenfranchised from safer living conditions that potentiated their risk of COVID-19 transmission and adverse outcomes. The lessons learned and shared among social service providers during the pandemic *(hopefully) will serve to improve future disaster responses for the people living without homes.*

ABSTRACTS *and Keywords*

CHAPTER ONE *Abstract*

Living Lives in Quiet Desperation

Abstract and Keywords: Social theorists, Habermas, theoretical conjectures, peripheral, social goods, domiciles

This study posits the needs and concerns of human beings: men, women, children, and families, living without domiciles, against the existing social politics and legislated public policy decisions affecting their daily lives. This qualitative research study has been written in four parts. Part One examines the objective experiences and the subjective responses of five homeless individuals living on the streets in a major southwestern city. Part Two consists of a search of the relevant sources of historical data affecting past and present legislated social welfare policies in the United States in the twentieth century. Part Three combines the welfare policy data with the interview data and analyzed through social theorists Jurgen Habermas, the feminist theorist Seyla Benhabib and care theorist Joan Tronto. Major federal laws and the states' interpretations of them are examined for their impact on the five individuals interviewed. Part Four will fast forward caring for the homeless to the present addressing the effects of the COVID-19 pandemic on the ability of the social services to meet critical needs of the people living homeless. The challenges and lessons learned from homeless service providers during this devastating pandemic will inform future responsibilities to care for men, women, children, and families facing COVID. Changes that are needed to help the people who are hopeless will be identified. How well are we complying as moral and ethical people?

Why am I qualified to write this book?

I have benefited from my education. It has helped me understand the homeless' situations on multiple levels. I have undergraduate degrees in both psychology and in sociology. My master's is in social work, and I have spent many hours in case management. Finally, my doctorate is in historical, social, and cultural studies in educational psychology. I understand how difficult it is for homeless people. They need more than financial handouts although money helps. They need help to get off the streets, out of the conundrum of their lives.

Why should you read this book?

There are many wonderful books available on homelessness. This textbook has an approach that is somewhat different.

First, my book offers in-depth, personal interviews with just five homeless people. I got to know them very well. I rode with them on the SEARCH mobile outreach van every week and sometimes daily.

Second, I have heard firsthand about their struggles with welfare personnel, policies, and laws.

Third, I have added the dimension of the social theorists Jurgen Habermas, Seyla Benhabib, (the ethics of social justice) and Joan Tronto, (the ethics of care). The homeless situation is examined considering its ethical treatment of the homeless people. There are basic expectations in our society for helping those who are suffering.

Fourth, Jurgen Habermas' theoretical conjectures on the lifeworld and the system explain why more people are sliding onto the streets, becoming more peripheral to the welfare system.

Fifth, this is the major argument in the book. It specifically uses the ethics of justice and the ethics of care when referencing the homeless. The community of others (citizens) do not understand that the people living without domiciles do not benefit from a "'just' distribution of social goods." They do not experience *social justice*. As was evident during the pandemic, the care homeless received was not *care informed by justice*.

Sixth, many homeless men, women, and children died during COVID-19. No one knew what to do with them in this crisis because they were not included in preplanning. The homeless concerns seem to have been put aside for more pressing concerns.

Seventh, Immanuel Kant wrote: "We have a duty to act morally." Is the care and concern we have and act on, in a crisis like COVID-19 toward the people living homeless, important?... Is it moral?

I hope graduating students will become advocates for the homeless. I am very aware that important disciplines such as social work, psychology, sociology, and public health need to have more classes about homelessness in graduate level student programs.

At the end of each chapter of the manuscript are exercises in **Critical Thinking.** These are entitled *Think Like Your Discipline*. If you are in a social work discipline, or a sociology discipline, a psychology or a public health discipline, or political science discipline you are asked to *engage intellectually* with your discipline. Develop a critical question for what you read in the chapter and then construct your own argument. Support your argument.

CHAPTER TWO *Abstract*

Privation of Ubiquitous Poverty.

Abstract and Keywords: unanchored, myths, privation, crisis poverty, the deserving and the undeserving poor, degradation rituals.

Privation of Ubiquitous Poverty. This phrase describes a concept of hidden and overlooked dimensions of poverty that are much more than material deprivation. This includes the lack of agency and control over their lives. Poverty is their constant daily struggle. Adding recalcitrant community social policies to their struggles for food, a bed, and their lives are stressful and challengingly difficult. This chapter begins with the discussion, "who are the homeless?" and "what causes it?" There are multiple causes. Poverty and no place to live are in first place. Not having any family to help them is another. Employment problems are exacerbated by the fact they do not have addresses and phone numbers. Additionally, with few job skills, plus no experience, finding and keeping a job is hard. They do not have transportation to get to jobs and they do not have childcare. Their treatment from many social welfare personnel is discussed as they are stigmatized and marginalized. Social conservatives are highly critical. They are accused of being the cause of their own homelessness.

CHAPTER THREE *Abstract*

Methodology for Qualitative Research

Abstract and keywords: marginalizing, stigmatization, predetermined criteria, purpose of study, qualitative, ontological.

Methodology for Qualitative Research. The purpose of this study is explained in this chapter. The research questions are identified. The method of choosing the five homeless people to be interviewed was based on predetermined criteria. The disadvantage of choosing only five people is that the results are limited and not as random. However, the answers received from the interviews are much more in depth and personal with this smaller group. Qualitative research interviewing methods were used with the study's predetermined questions. Ontological interviewing was used with some people. Interviewing began after consent forms were signed.

Interview questions:

a. Can you tell me briefly about your life?
b. What circumstances have resulted in your life on the street?
c. What has been the hardest for you?
d. How long have you been homeless?
e. How are you managing?
f. Do you want to participate in the study?
g. Are you sober from drugs and alcohol?
h. Can you understand the questions?
i. What do you believe are the attitudes of those who are not homeless towards you?

Donnie had a brief interview to be finished later. Bill was the first full interviewee.

CHAPTER FOUR *Abstract*

The slide to full homelessness.

Abstract and keywords: tramp trail, mental instability, learned helplessness/ learned hopelessness, existential crisis, moral imperative.

The slide to full homelessness. The research social worker rode in the mobile outreach van with the coordinator looking for homeless camps for people in need. During the daily rides, five homeless people were identified for the study; and some were interviewed. Those interviewed were Willie, the dishwasher, Donnie, the gentleman, Billy, just hanging out, Robbie, a shopping cart woman, and the orphan, Bill. They discussed how they became homeless, and how they have been treated by some front-line social service personnel.

Willie's behavior showed learned helplessness that had turned to learned hopelessness. He had a lack of social power and could not really interact with non-homeless people. Donnie talked about the *tramp trail* and Billy displayed his animosity (his word). He almost demanded to be heard when he said, "we all be human." Billy demonstrated, like others living homeless, that he was somewhat mentally unstable. He had grown up on and off the streets. People growing up in homelessness can become emotionally unanchored. He said he did not feel like he belonged anywhere. Donnie was experiencing an *existential crisis*. He wanted to be able to live to a *moral imperative*. A moral imperative is a strongly held principle that compels one to act in a certain way. He did not want to be considered homeless.

CHAPTER FIVE *Abstract*

Existing Emotionally Unanchored.

Abstract and keywords: pet peeves, meaninglessness, intolerant social service personnel, criminalization, hierarchy, emotionally unanchored.

Existing Emotionally Unanchored. Without stable domiciles people exist with emotional difficulty. In this chapter the mobile outreach coordinator describes the social system in the camps. The higher-functioning homeless people help others. There is a hierarchy like a family. The coordinator addresses the rules of available shelters which have become his pet peeves. Problems the homeless have with intolerant front-line social services personnel are discussed. These reflect prejudices, stereotyping, and beliefs that the person living as they do is a social deviant or a criminal. They are told they are criminals for sleeping in doorways and in full sight: when they have no place else to rest. They are blamed and told their poverty is their own fault. Women are blamed for depending on a man or they are blamed for not having a man. They are told they should have a job but with no childcare they are not able to work. They avoid going to the welfare offices and asking for help because they are treated with contempt.

CHAPTER SIX *Abstract*

Hegemony is the Tyranny of the Majority.

Abstract and keywords: overt social policies, covert exclusion, public degradation rituals, hegemony, community ordinances.

Hegemony is the Tyranny of the Majority. This chapter describes the different cultural ideologies in the United States. Federal money is disbursed to the states who give different amounts to the homeless. Traditionalistic, moralistic, and paternalistic ideologies of the states determine the amount dispersed. There is no equity.

Many state policies are covertly exclusionary and promote racism. The poor cannot influence welfare policy. A voice is needed to speak for the homeless to express what they need. The bottom line for welfare is how well it addresses real needs. Policies are tolerated that punish the person living homeless. The homeless persons' life circumstances leave them no choice but to exist in full sight of others. Anti-homeless community ordinances serve to punish and to make their lives more difficult. Public rituals degrade vulnerable people. Homeless are picked up and taken out of the cities and dropped off some place. Police go into camps like the one Bill was in and gather up all the homeless' possessions. They then take them to the dumpster, leaving the homeless even more destitute. When citizens disagree about the morality of public policies, it is because they cannot put themselves in the homeless person's place. They do not see them as human beings needing help.

CHAPTER SEVEN *Abstract*

Welfare State Bureaucracies

Abstract and keywords: Anti-homeless ordinances, implicit social policies, existential crisis, policy's intent, degrading, discrimination, equal distribution.

Welfare State Bureaucracies. This chapter discusses pertinent welfare policies since the Great Depression. It addresses ordinances that are anti-homeless and implicit policies that cause existential crises for the homeless. The anti-homeless ordinances in different large cities around the U.S. are identified. The difficulties in applying for welfare policies are found to be degrading and humiliating for the homeless. The intent of the policies is overshadowed by the negative ways they are presented. People are dropped from welfare at their neediest times. This happens with the change in presidential administrations. When they are dropped from welfare rolls, they are left with nothing to fall back on to take its place. Politicians believe they can get jobs to replace what is taken away. They cannot and even if they do it does not begin to cover what was lost.

CHAPTER EIGHT *Abstract*

The System Uncouples from the Lifeworld.

Abstract and keywords: Habermas, milieu, uncoupling of system and lifeworld, ontologically formal worlds, lifeworld, pathologies of a bourgeois society, anomie, existential crisis

The System Uncouples from the Lifeworld. This chapter discusses the social theorist Jurgen Habermas' theoretical constructs of the system and the lifeworld. This chapter is very relevant addressing how homeless people become homeless, and why they remain. The longer the homeless person lives the life separated from normal society the more he experiences anomie and an existential crisis.

Culture, society, and people are discussed as the structural components of the lifeworld. As money and power drive the system, people living homeless become more peripheral to a system that has grown past them. During the COVID-19 pandemic, homeless people suffered because there were no emergency plans in place for how to take care of them during a crisis.

Habermas conjectured that as the complexity of the system increases, so does the lifeworld… becoming less important. Living separated from meaningful others, one compensates by moving into a world of disorder, senselessness and madness. Durkheim wrote that the "I is only understood in the context of a We."

Donnie is a homeless man interviewed. He talked at length about his life. He stated he did not know the purpose of his life. His identity and his reality were transforming into an existential crisis. What he had to look forward to was his social security at age 62 and going fishing. He lived an existence in quiet despair and loneliness.

CHAPTER NINE *Abstract*
An Ethic of Justice Informs an Ethic of Care

Abstract and keywords: System, rationalization of the lifeworld, uncoupling of system and lifeworld, position-take, theory of discourse ethics.

An Ethic of Justice Informs an Ethic of Care. This chapter addresses the basic theoretical constructs that appear throughout this book. What represents the good and what is undesirable in our society is seen through an ethic of justice and an ethic of care in our treatment of the homeless. The question of justice appears when the homeless are subjected to new welfare policies. These policies were thought to end poverty but have made the lives of the homeless more difficult. The care they are receiving has been reduced exponentially with each new presidential administration.

The fundamental nature of caring is "position-taking" with the recipient. The theory of discourse ethics charges the moral responsibility of those designing welfare policies with acquiring more knowledge and understanding of the needs of homeless people. Homeless people are unable to negotiate for policies to meet their real needs because they lack political agency.

The rationalization of the lifeworld means the lives of the homeless become less important to a system's functioning. The homeless become peripheral to the system. The welfare policies meet their needs less and less as they move farther away from the system. As the system's complexity grows, the lifeworld is further reduced, becoming less important to the functioning of the system.

CHAPTER TEN *Abstract*

Before and After COVID-19 Pandemic.
Abstract and keywords: delimit, defining boundaries, good welfare reform, care of versus caretaking, generalized other, the concrete other.

Before and After COVID-19 Pandemic. Even with face-to-face dialogue the homeless were peripheral to concerns that social politics described during the COVID-19 pandemic. The people living homeless were subjected to less than dignity-supporting attitudes by social welfare front-line personnel who were themselves struggling. This chapter addresses the generalized and the concrete other. The generalized other represents broader societal norms. The concrete other pertains to personal interactions and recognition of individuality. This chapter demonstrates how the ethical considerations in justice and care apply to the COVID-19 pandemic and the homeless caught up in fear, sickness, and confusion.

CHAPTER ELEVEN *Abstract*

Politics, the Means to Achieve Moral Ends?

Abstract and keywords: Public and private, power differentials, Universalistic Moral Theory, the otherness of the other, degradation rituals.

This chapter addresses the generalized other and the concrete other. For those in the community who want to care for the homeless, they must 'position-take.' This means they must put themselves in the place of the homeless to feel what they feel to appreciate their situation. They then must decide to act. This chapter shows the separation of the public and private, or justice from care. Degradation rituals transform an individual's identity or status to a lower position within a group. Social service personnel who are on the front lines are aware of power differentials between themselves and homeless people. It is not hard to understand that they may have been in the same position as the homeless at one time.

CHAPTER TWELVE *Abstract*

"We Have a Duty to Act Morally."

Abstract and keywords: duty, moral obligations, paternalistic

We Have a Duty to Act Morally. This chapter highlights Immanuel Kant's conjectures about our duty as citizens and as moral people. Kant believes we have moral obligations whether we want them or not. We must cultivate our conscience. As moral people, we need to be aware of our paternalistic lack of respect when we press some social welfare policies, on unwilling homeless people. For it to be a good social policy it must be in their social interest. If it is offered to them compassionately and with concern it will not be dignity-denying. Ethical principles like beneficence, nonmaleficence, autonomy, and justice are central to consistently creating a lasting framework that becomes part of our social conscience.

CHAPTER ONE

Living Lives in Quiet Desperation

Introduction

Many citizens act out of guilt toward the homeless. They offer old clothes, food on holidays, and the occasional blanket when it is cold. Although these items are critically needed, homeless people need more than clothes and food. They need the experience of home. Existentially, an inner sense of *unheimlich*, not "at home" affects them subjectively. Home is a metaphor expressing inclusion in the life of a family and a community; when one has no home, one is displaced (Hudson, 1998). Home is more than shelter. Home has deeper meaning and only begins with shelter from unkindness. It incorporates familiarity, comfort, and a safety net shielding from a multiplicity of assaults of the world. It means someone cares about them (Pustejovsky, 2002).

Poverty is always there, always hanging over everything. A solution must start with the community's social politics and the willingness of citizens to change their attitudes toward people living homeless and welfare policies.

CHAPTER TWO

Privation of Ubiquitous Poverty

The battered mobile outreach van searches the city for homeless people needing help. The coordinator and the researcher walked down the steep slope to the bayou. On one side was a concrete wall of varying heights. There was evidence of pee-mark stains. Here men stood facing the wall for months or years, some were merely dirty while others were black perhaps indicating blood in their urine. As they walked, they came up to an area with thousands of cigarette butts, cans, paper, clothes, and empty fast-food cartons. The smells of accumulated human existence permeated the area. Deep under the culvert at a distance, lying on a sloping concrete bed, they saw a huge African American man. He was lying exactly perpendicular to an eight-foot wall rising above him. On the ledge, carefully placed directly over his sleeping head was a metal robot with menacing red eyes, a child's toy. Placed as a warning to anyone coming up on him. This sign caused the group to pause at a distance. The message was unmistakable. The man was acutely mentally ill and when the coordinator asked him if he needed anything, he glared at them, so effectively that they immediately put down the water and sandwiches and left.

People living without domiciles are seen in full sight of others. Today this man was found on the set of concrete culverts supporting bridges lining Buffalo Bayou. Here was a jungle of dirt, weeds, and bushes providing a perfect hiding place for the man on the labyrinth of concrete. The man was easily identified as a homeless man.

Definition of Homelessness

The Steward B. McKinney Homeless Assistance Act, of 1987 defined homelessness as a defining trait of an individual. That is,

(1) "people/individuals who lack a fixed, regular, and adequate nighttime residence and includes a subset for an individual who is exiting an institution where he or she resided for 90 days or less and who resided in an emergency shelter,

(2) a place not meant for human habitation immediately before entering that institution.

(3) individuals and families who imminently lose their primary nighttime residence,

(4) unaccompanied youth and families with children and youth who are defined as homeless under other federal statutes who do not otherwise qualify as homeless under this definition,

5) individuals and families who are fleeing, or are attempting to flee, domestic violence, dating violence, sexual assault, stalking, or other dangerous or life-threatening conditions that relate to violence against the individual or a family member."

However, recently Rodriguez, et.al. in a 2021 BMC Public Health article #1657, identified homelessness as a "state that is experienced, one that is amenable to intervention." This definition positions homeless people as being willing for help and open and responsive to being assisted in finding a place to live, get a job and have transportation. The word amenable when used with the homeless suggests that they are willing to cooperate and adapt.

Human beings living homeless are recognized from the impoverished settings, the context of their very public lives, and the culturally recognizable patterns of their behavior. Seventy-five percent of the people living homeless are single, unattached adults without children. Men outnumber women five-to-one. Families headed by single mothers with children comprise another twenty percent. The remaining 5% percent consists of adolescents. The average age of unattached homeless adults is middle to late thirties with a small portion considered elderly (50 and up) by the Department of Housing and Urban Development (HUD). Forty percent of the total homeless are African American and the rest are Anglo with small numbers of Hispanic and Asian. Many homeless adults have histories of institutional confinement in jails, prisons, or psychiatric hospitals. Fifty percent of all homeless adult populations are diagnosed with current or past alcohol and drug use problems.

Causes of Homelessness

Beliefs about the causes of poverty and homelessness lie at the root of many of our most important social welfare policies (Burch,1991). Those beliefs are (1) the poor will always exist, (2) their poverty is their fault, but we still need to help them, (3) they have just had bad luck, and (4) it is the fault of society. Whether these represent valid understandings or not, homelessness does not happen in a vacuum and there is no single cause. Lack of housing, psychiatric disability, substance abuse, domestic violence, and chronic illness, all to one extent or another predict the future likelihood of homelessness. However, poverty is the common denominator.

With increasing housing rentals, destruction of low-income housing, cuts in federal housing programs, and changes in the implementation of federal welfare law, the number of people living without homes is presently increasing. Individuals and families existing on the margins between living domiciled or living without a place to call their home can slip into homelessness when affected by a sluggish economy, a rising jobless rate, and a natural disaster such as the COVID-19 pandemic.

The poor have not had a voice to influence policy decisions affecting the distribution of goods and services to them. Their needs are assumed, and they are not given the opportunity to express their real needs. Covert policies promote institutional racism, sexism, and classism (Burch,1991). These policies overemphasize social inclusion but tolerate covert exclusion.

"The others" are excluded while promoting the "tyranny of the majority" (Everingham, 2001).

The privation surrounding the lives of homeless individuals consists both of economic problems as well as the lack of extended family to support their attempts to stay employed. Unlike the 'hobos' of times past, when it was (arguably) perceived that they "chose" this life, most homeless individuals and families today would choose very different circumstances (Burch, 1991). In a nation in which social honor, prestige, self-respect, and quality of life are all linked, poor people and the homeless are viewed as responsible for their life conditions. They are disrespected and blamed for continuing to live as they do and this negative view and the gap between early aspirations and the real opportunities available to them perpetuates their homelessness. Finally, besides social, and economic considerations exacerbating living without domiciles, aspects of federal welfare law and state discretionary implementation of welfare policy have worked together to effectively shift at-risk populations into homelessness. Cutbacks in social spending have occurred as the result of federal, state and local social politics being unwilling to address the real needs of the impoverished. States have been given funds to distribute to qualified homeless people. The states have put those funds in state bank accounts earning interest while the homeless survive on less. However, overall, the lack of available housing and the persistence of poverty are the primary factors causing homelessness (Halter, 1995).

Employment

Employment opportunities for the homeless are limited because of the lack of job skills, transportation, and minimal human capital restricting the types of jobs they can find with sufficient earnings to support themselves. Even when they attain jobs, the minimum wage does not cover even the cost of federally funded housing (Halter,1995). Jobs that they might be qualified for have been denied because they cannot give a home address or a telephone number. Additionally, they have no transportation to get to the job. They are stereotyped as criminals, drunks, bums, and prostitutes becoming some of the most stigmatized citizens in our society (Goffman, 1963; Anderson, Snow, & Cress, 1994; Levy, 1999; Oyserman, 2001; Phelan, et al., 1997).

Blaming the Victims

In general, when others consider people in the lower classes, they blame the victims by focusing on their apparent disabling orientation to the present or by the perception of their inability to delay gratification. Social service agency personnel complain that the homeless are unwilling to plan or wait their turn. Homeless individuals wait to seek welfare support until they are desperately in need of some sort of immediate assistance. Many hold off because the experience of interacting with many social service agency personnel is disheartening and dignity-denying. A person living homeless is considered undeserving (Gulati, 1990).

Even social welfare personnel participate in the marginalizing and stereotyping of these vulnerable human beings. While some welfare individuals do not say much, the homeless person can read the contempt the worker may have for them in the worker's face. While this puts the homeless off from pursuing welfare assistance, the homeless person has learned to ignore the pain that this causes and continue until they get their needs met. This is a large reason the homeless person waits until they need help. The experience with the welfare personnel and many others is called the degradation ritual.

Conservative scholars have proposed a distinction should be made between the *deserving poor* and the *undeserving poor* and this distinction should inform public policy (Meade, 1989; Gulati, 1990). Meade (1989) argued that granting government entitlements, where nothing is expected in return, shields recipients from the "treats and the rewards" of the system. Included in this argument were women and children who were viewed as responsible for their fate. These conservative researchers have argued the impoverished condition of women is the direct result of depending on welfare instead of on a man. Any woman, they have suggested, who depends on government subsidies and not on her earnings is always depending on someone. She will always be "*one man away from welfare*" (Jencks, 1992).

C. Wright Mills wrote of private troubles and public issues as those troubles occurring within the character of the individual. (Logoff & Fieldstone, 2000, p. 2). Mills wrote that helping the poor hurts them in the long run and having a job is good for them. These people, conservative scholars argue, must be forced to work by the withdrawal of government social aid (Jencks, 1992). The problems are many with this attitude, and only begin with lack of skills but more importantly not knowing how to act in a work environment. The fallacy in this attitude is the only thing these homeless people have is a subsidy from the government. When this is taken from them, they are thrown into a cauldron of lack and distress. They slide further on to the streets.

Other research has made the distinction between the *chronically needy* and the *transitionally needy*. Chronically needy welfare recipients are the "truly needy" who, due to medical or social difficulties, are unable to work. The transitionally needy are considered able to work and are eligible to receive cash benefits for a limited amount of time. The concern remains, however, that these transitionally needy people will become dependent on welfare as an alternative to getting a job. Therefore, it was determined that a work incentive is needed. The prevailing social politics in many areas of the country support removing people from welfare rolls, thus placing them into the position of having to find a job to live. When they cannot find a job, they exist without shelter and food. Having not been in this untenable situation, detached social others use myths to explain and rationalize, to themselves and others. Their beliefs are that the needy should be able to take advantage of the "opportunity" of experiencing the economic independence gained from having a job. Detached social others have no real understanding of what is involved (Halter, 1995).

Myth

Many people cling to the myths surrounding the homeless. They believe the homeless actively avoid taking advantage of the "opportunity" of economic independence because they want to live as they do. Myths enable others to make sense of what they do not understand in their world. These invented stories help to explain the behavior of others not like us who do not adhere to normative, socially acceptable behavior. Jurgen Habermas wrote, "Men are compelled to impose a meaningful order upon reality," thus, plausible, invented stories serve to fix understanding (Habermas, 1973, p. 118).

Myths are founded upon and continue to exist as expressions of the collective social psyche and are interpreted to reach an understanding of society's problems. This is accomplished in much the same way that a dream is interpreted for an individual (Golden, 2000). Historically, traditional societies were based on accepted dichotomies between royalty and common folks, aristocracy and the non-aristocratic, priests and laymen, and freeman and serf. These contradictions were justified as reflections of the hierarchical order of things, grounding their identification with the society in which they lived (Taylor, 1979). Modern society, however, has become homogenized. Even with varied socio-economic levels, citizens can develop *a* unity of outlook and lifestyle (p. 111). This unification happens less as the distance increases between socioeconomic levels. In a society where everyone is expected to be like the dominant group, out-groups do not participate fully in the decisions affecting society. (2215)

THINK LIKE YOUR DISCIPLINE...Critical thinking. #2
Critical thinking involves deeply analyzing a subject from the chapter. Learn to read critically. Develop some assumptions and question them. Then evaluate your position. By considering and responding to opposing viewpoints, thus strengthening your understanding. You may ask each other's assumptions but don't use the same subject from the chapter. Use a class period to listen to other viewpoints.

CHAPTER THREE

Qualitative Research Methods

The methodology of this research is composed of two parts: Part one consists of interviews with five homeless people living on the streets. Data was collected over several weeks many times while riding in the SEARCH outreach van. Part two ontological interviewing was incorporated.

The research began and ended with concern for the men, women, and children who are living homeless on the streets of a major southwest city in Texas. Questions were asked in a friendly, relaxed atmosphere encouraging the person interviewed to talk with the researcher. Open-ended questions yielded, what their life was like living without a domicile. The person being interviewed was treated respectfully and gently.

The researcher sought to find out from them if they felt like they had been stigmatized. They nodded their heads and generally did not answer. This subject brought up the pain of not being considered good enough. The researcher gently supported them and moved on to other questions. Did the person living homeless feel they received care from the community of others that was just and right? They were generally unsure whether they did or did not. The researcher got the impression they did not know if the care they received was appropriate.

Mission of SEARCH

The mission of the SEARCH Homeless Project is to respond to the needs of people living without domiciles by providing opportunities to change their lives. An effort was made to enhance their dignity and self-worth. The mobile outreach program began in 1992 responding to the needs of those unaware of or unable to access the SEARCH services or the services of other social service providers.

Goals of Outreach Team

The goals of the outreach team were (1) to locate areas where unsheltered homeless individuals congregate or camp; (2) to determine their service needs; (3) to take needed services to these homeless individuals and families; (4) and to act as a liaison for other service providers to access this indigent population.

The outreach team regularly covered a large area and was constantly concerned that they did not have enough time or personnel to reach all the homeless in need in this large area. The outreach team consisted of the coordinator, a case manager, a drug and alcohol counselor, a nurse practitioner, and other technicians and professionals who rode in the van with the team at different times. The team drove out every morning and afternoon six days a week, sometimes continuing into the evening hours. The white, rather battered van identified the team as being from SEARCH Homeless Services and when the homeless see it, they know there is, at the very least, food and water to be given out.

Homeless people were observed over several weeks. Five were interviewed two times each. The people interviewed were randomly chosen using qualitative research methods. The homeless participants were chosen based on their availability and accessibility. The disadvantage of this method was that those chosen may not have represented the broader population of the SEARCH homeless. They were encountered naturally over the days and week's outreach efforts. This method has been used when sampling for marginalized groups.

Criteria for inclusion in study

The criteria used for inclusion in the study were whether the person demonstrated orientation to time, place, and person. As a licensed Master of Social Work and a licensed chemical dependency counselor, the researcher (Marilyn) was careful to evaluate them for rational thinking, acceptable sobriety, and a managed mental illness. Depending on how long they had been living as they were, there were varying levels of cognitive awareness and connection to reality. The longer a homeless person lived on the streets, the more opportunity he had of being affected by isolation and loneliness. The environment they live in, their personal struggles, and their concerns about living as they do, take a toll over time on their mental health. Evidence of violent tendencies in some people is known by the coordinator. Those agreeing to the interview were assured of their anonymity as well as the confidentiality of their answers. Their permanent location would never be revealed in the final report.

What is the purpose of the research?

The purpose of the research was carefully explained, and it was to hear from the homeless people themselves what they needed. This is an attempt to eventually influence welfare policies to benefit individuals living without domiciles. Five homeless people were interviewed to find out directly from each of them what their needs were. They were encouraged to speak up about those needs. They were asked while riding in the SEARCH mobile van a couple of times. They were asked for the information in different ways.

Current social welfare policy has been designed for them without consulting them. They appreciated being asked for their opinions. They were instructed, if they had any questions to ask the coordinator to contact Marilyn, the research social worker. The researcher employed interviewing techniques that encouraged them to identify their feelings about their situations. Ontological interviewing was employed.

Donnie

Ontological techniques of interviewing were the focus. In these qualitative interviews, objective facts were not the total goal. The additional goals were the subjective meaning of the interviewee's lived realities. Donnie was asked questions directly. He was determined by the researcher to be the highest functioning person of the group of five. He was in the best position to understand some of the more difficult questions. Others had trouble with understanding.

Foundational questions:
1. What are your housing needs?
2. What are your income inadequacies?
3. What is your access to healthcare support?
4. What conversations do you have with your children about your situation?
5. What address do you put on job applications?

Of the foundational questions the only one he wanted to answer was about his problem finding and sustaining a house or an apartment that was his. He did not feel he was disconnected from society, he felt society had disconnected from him. He does not talk with his grown children because he said they ignore him. Finally, and most sadly, he did not look for an apartment or a room that could be his because he did not have an address or telephone number to put on the application. He knew he would be rejected. He wanted to avoid humiliation at all costs.

Subjective questions:
1. How do you define your disconnection from society? (disconnection in the context of homelessness)
2. What aspects of your identity have changed?
3. Do you have a sense of belonging?
4. What have you lost due to homelessness?
5. How do people's attitudes toward homelessness affect you?

The rest of the subjective questions he had trouble with or tried to avoid answering them. He did say that he was wounded (my supplied word) by the attitudes of people when they realized he was homeless, despite his neat haircut and trimmed beard. Donnie stated that he did not feel he belonged anywhere, and he felt he had lost the respect of his children.

I asked Donnie what he thought was the meaning of his life. He was quiet for several seconds then he lowered his head and shook it back and forth saying "I don't know. I don't know."

Donnie usually fell back on his old daydream. In his mind all his problems would be over once he got his social security. The subjective meaning of the lived realities of his life were that he struggled to keep his bed in the resource center. Donnie was haunted by the question that the social worker asked him. What was the meaning of his life? Donnie thought, hell he had no idea. He sometimes thought about his ex-wife and his daughter but not often. Long ago he got used to being lonely for meaningful interaction. He avoided interactions with the homeless people around him. He created and sustained his reality. His life revolved around his schedule: getting in line for bed, getting up at 7:00 in the morning, meals. He became somewhat paralyzed by his routine. He kept to himself out of fear of being treated badly, a victim of the violence that was prevalent on the streets against older homeless people.

Bill

I asked another man, Bill, one question about how his identity may or may not have changed since living as he does. He looked sad and said slowly, "I used to see myself differently. I was proud to be a concert violinist. Today, I don't know. It is not as good, not as good." Bill went on to say that he received negative looks from non-homeless people. Most of the time they pretended that he did not exist. He had a place to live but he felt isolated and alienated from the rest of the world. He did not talk much, and he did not have anything but a few friends in the camp. He said that he felt pushed to the edge of the "world" (his word.) And interestingly, he felt his life was like being trapped in a labyrinth (my word offered). When the social worker asked him what he meant, he said that he was lost in the complexities (my word) of life.

Observations/Interviews:

The battered mobile outreach van once again "searched" the city and county for homeless individuals who need help. They did this repeatedly every day. They are offered bottled water, sandwiches, fruit or orange juice, medical care, and a ride to the hospital or treatment. The first day riding with the outreach team we pulled up to concrete culverts supporting a series of bridges just at the northern edge of downtown. The coordinator, the case manager, and the researcher got out of the van and walked into the labyrinth of concrete, dirt, weeds, and bushes lining Buffalo Bayou. Coming out of the wall at a large open culvert was a large pipe about 100 inches in diameter. Water was draining from the street above. The coordinator said homeless men and women used it as a shower and since it had just rained, the water was clean.

As we walked, the coordinator described the social system he had observed in the camps once set up here. When there are five or more people in the group, one or two hold the group together. They are the most highly functioning and the easiest to get into different services. However, when they leave the group, the rest of the camp will dissipate. These higher-functioning ones keep everyone in food, beer, drugs, or whatever and they take care of the group. When these caretakers leave, then the whole situation of the group will change, and the rest will move on to the place where they find another caretaker.

We searched this area and came up with a dirty place much farther and deeper under the concrete culverts. Here there was evidence of human inhabitance with thousands of cigarette butts, cans, paper, clothes, and empty fast-food food containers littering the area. The smells of accumulated human existence pervaded the area. Deep under the culvert at a distance, we saw three homeless men lying at different angles to an eight-foot wall rising above them. They became aware of us and were angered at the intrusion. We left immediately, leaving the rest of the bottled water and sandwiches.

INTERVIEWS CONTINUING

Bill: The Orphan

I was introduced to Bill when he rode in the mobile outreach van. He had been described to me beforehand as a mobile outreach team success story. Through their concerted efforts, Bill received treatment and medication, a small apartment, and he applied for and received SSI to live on. He appeared to me to be a small, vulnerable person inside of an adult body and I was very much aware that he had for a time been a concert violinist with a master's degree in music. I smiled at him and reminded him we had talked earlier.

Marilyn: "Please call me Marilyn. Can I call you Bill?"
Bill looked down but nodded his head.
Marilyn: "Do you mind if I ask you some very informal questions?
Bill: "No, not a bit."
Marilyn: "How old are you?"
Bill: "57. I will be tomorrow."
Marilyn: "Tomorrow! Well, Happy Birthday! (with much enthusiasm) How long have you been living at SEARCH?"
Bill: "Uh…pause I moved to Houston in '69, uh… 31 years."
Marilyn: "How long have you been homeless?" (said gently).
Bill: "Oh", (he pauses) "about ten years."

Marilyn: "What uh set of…uh…events or circumstances in your life led you to live homeless?"

Bill: "Uh…uh…I lost ma job and…uh…I didn't have any money to pay for a place to stay anymore."

Marilyn: "Ohhhhh, that's hard." (Said gently and compassionately). "Do you have any family down here?"

Bill: "No, (said quickly) I have very few in Oregon. I haven't been in touch with them for years."

Marilyn: "That is probably going to happen with my sisters," I said this to try to connect and to relieve the tightness I had created in the interview.

Bill laughs, "Ha ha ha HAHAHA…" (starting quietly, rising to a louder laugh.)

I had the sense that this had become a connecting moment. He understood that I understood.

Bill: "My Aunt wrote me a letter a year ago (he breaks in, clearly into talking). Her nephew found my address on the Internet on a site for the homeless to connect with family…pause. I guess they wanted to see if I was the right (says his name). I never answered her."

(I then interrupted him. Immediately, I stopped.)

Bill: "HUH? Oh, well that her nephew, (voice gets louder and brighter) …what I just said about finding out whether I was the right person or not." Bill had submitted his name to an Internet site for homeless people, hoping someone would care enough to look for him. He seemed to be saying, 'Isn't it ridiculous that after all these years someone cared enough to find me?'

Bill: "She said she would give me my mother's wedding ring. But I…"

(I interrupt again.)

Marilyn:" Oh your mother is not alive anymore."

Bill: "Oh, my mother has been dead most of my life." (said in a lifted lilting voice) "I was four." (said quietly). "My maiden aunt, she and my grandfather, they raised me."

(Long pause, but for once I keep my mouth shut.)

Bill: "I missed my mother. We were out shopping, and she had a heart attack. They took her to the doctor's office. I could not understand why she could not come home. I said, "I will be good, I promise I will be good if she will come home.""

He says this rapidly, louder, with feeling. I could easily feel this experience; feeling the pain that was still there after all these years. I felt very sad for the little boy who still resides deep in this grown man.

Marilyn: "Is it hard to talk about this today?"

Bill: "Oh, I don't have any feelings about it. It was bad, I guess."

(A long pause)

After his mother's death, Bill lived with relatives. He lived a life emotionally unanchored to those around him, Habermas, (1984). Bill's memories were stored in what Habermas named the *lifeworld*. One can never step out of one's lifeworld. All new experiences and understandings are stored, formed, and layered upon one another. This correlates the understandings we have with others. It stabilizes identities. It is produced throughout life, and it is from this reservoir we blend with others in our daily lives. It is the background horizon of our lives. When it is formed on uncertainty, lack of structure, and constant poverty, the individual may exist *emotionally unanchored* to his world (Lewin, 2000). It appeared that after his mother's death, Bill lived with uncertainty and constant poverty. It is not surprising that Bill continued to live unconnected.

Marilyn: "Have you lived in a tent or other domicile since you have been living homeless?"

Bill: "Yeah. There was one old man that I used to stay with when I was out on the streets. Or he stayed in the camp with us. He always had sores all over his arms and I remember that SEARCH came out with a medical doctor to look at the sores one time. They got him a ride to go to the clinic. He was a very timid man, and he sat all day in the clinic and never saw anyone. At 10:00 at night he was still sitting there. This old man lived in my camp with me. Or I lived with him. He died of a heart attack."

Marilyn: "With you, when you were there?"

Bill: "Well, yes. He was making a homestead for him and me. He came home from selling newspapers one evening. He wanted to lie down, and I found him lying across the bed." (Pause)

Bill: "I lay down by him and hoped that he would wake up soon. I was shocked. I did not know what I was doing." (His voice changes.) 2,555

INTERVIEWS CONTINUING

WILLIE: The Dishwasher

Amid scores of people in the SEARCH resource center and the laughter and arguments, of 150 men, Willie was interviewed. He was very humble. Willie worked as the dishwasher and was proud of his job. The clinical director of the center asked him if he would be willing to talk with me. Sitting close enough to hear one another, in a far corner of the room, we proceeded. Willie was friendly and willing to answer questions. Comments are using his own grammar.

Marilyn: "Tell me a little bit about when you were a child. Did you live in Houston?"

Willie: "Well, I was born in Louisiana in Shreveport. I left Shreveport when I was seven with my grandmother. I been to a lot of places. I been mainly here. I have one sister."

Marilyn: "Does she live in Houston?"

Willie: "Yes, mam, but not lately. I been dodging her. We had a misunderstanding. I have been talking to her on the phone but mainly I been dodging her."

Marilyn: "…because she wants you to … uh…"

Willie: "She don't appreciate the life I am livin…but like I told her, I'm 58, I don't have no education, I have seizures, and I can't work like others. I tell them I have seizures, once I tell them that they don't want me."

Born into poverty, Willie had been living on the margins of society all his life. His lived realities of his life growing up in a time of pronounced segregation, he saw himself as uneducated, unskilled, and seizure ridden. Willie appeared to have rejected the place society assigned for him in life. He preferred to avoid community control (i.e., sister control) and he lived around others with whom he felt equal.

Willie grew up depositing negative views of himself in his lifeworld. He deposited the cultural/societal beliefs and expectations conveyed from previous generations of his family and in multiple attitudes of white people toward him, a black child, then man. Additionally, his identity was formed from the reflections he had seen of himself in other's faces. From his childhood to his present conception of himself, he had developed a sense of who he thought he was and compared himself with others, very negatively. What he felt was he was very much less than others. He felt that he never did measure up, and he stayed "hidden" from others in the homeless life. His health and seizures were a source of shame.

Marilyn: "Have you had seizures ever since you were a child?"

Willie: "No mum, I had an aneurism about twenty years ago that busted in ma head."

Marilyn: "Oh my God!"

Willie: "After that I had seizures. It is brought on mostly by stress.

I had a seizure about a week ago. You can only live here so long, and I was wondering where I was going to go after this. That night I went to bed thinking about that and the next morning I had a seizure so. . .".

Marilyn: "So where are you living now?"

Willie: "I can stay in the shelter until January. After January I guess I will be on the streets somewhere. Got to go somewhere."

Marilyn: "Can you come in here (the SEARCH Resource Center)? I don't know how that works".

Willie: "Yeah…in here it is for school and job preparation, not just to stay. But they try to help me as much as they can. What I am trying to do now is find someone who will let me work with my seizures and all… because I filed for SSI and… uh…I don't know how that going' go and I can't depend on it, and I got to find me a job and take care of myself. So, I'm waiting on SSI and I'm waiting on a job."

Marilyn: "Now, is anyone helping you with getting SSI?"

Willie: "Who goin' help me? No mum, Gulf Coast Legal Aid. I filed with them, and the man came here every Thursday, and I filed with him in September. They lost my file, and he is trying to relocate my file."

Marilyn: "They lost your file." (incredulous)

Willie: "So, what they did, they made MHMRA the payee and they sent them a letter for me to come to court. MHMRA did not give me the letter. They canceled it and I must go through the entire process again."

Willie: The Court did not call so we call them. The man said, "Oh yeah in the letter it stated that refusal to come to court"… tol' them, "how can I come to court if I didn't get no letter?"

Willie: "The guy says it's not their fault and I had to start all over again. I had a $1,600 savings account in MHMRA from some of my SSI checks. I told them I needed that money. They told me I could not use that, I had to go to Social Security. I went to Social Security and told them and the man at Social Security told me to go back to MHMRA and tell them to give me the money because it is between Social Security and me. I went back and told the guy at MHMRA. and he said, no, we do not want no trouble."

Marilyn: "When was this?"

Willie: "About two years ago. Ever since then, I been volunteering but I don't make any money but it…sometimes I get some. I cannot get no room or nuthin' because I do not know if I get no work or not.

Willie: "It was a counselor; they was the payee. See, like you are homeless, you don't have no education- you don't know what to do. You can't hire you no lawyer, you can go down there to Legal Aid but they ain't goin' represent you as a lawyer would. OK, now a man met me on the streets and said, "I pay you $15 if you know where to buy some drugs." I told him you can go up there around the corner and you can find drugs. He found the drugs, he an undercover, they come back and arrest me and I goin' to prison for two years. I had the sentence reduced to 6 months but while I was there, they came to me and say I bought a pistol in '61 and it was used in a robbery, and I was a murderer. They give me two more years for that. It wasn't my gun, I ain't no murderer. They knew that; they needed to pin it on someone."

Marilyn: "How do you deal with that?"

Willie: "I just grit my teeth and keep going. Because you know there ain't nuthin' I can do about that cause it takes money to fight em. It kinda like trying to fight a gang they ain't goin to give you nothing but they goin' take everything from you. I come out and try to start all over. That was in 1989."

Willie's treatment by almost everyone having more social power than he does effectively subjugates him. Willie long ago adopted an attitude of learned helplessness and has added to it, learned hopelessness to tolerate his life.

Universal, abstract principles of what is *just* can be applied here and are meaningless. Of course, this is not *just*, but it is perpetuated by too little money to hire too few people to offer care. Along with too little care, he was subjected to attitudes of service personnel at the welfare office, Social Security and legal aid discouraging him from trying harder. He just gave up pushing harder to be heard.

> **Marilyn:** "The social politics on the streets are good and bad. What have you observed of others?"

> > **Willie:** "It has been up and down. When you are out there, you learn everybody out there for themselves; they got the crack and everything. When I was growing up everyone looked out for each other. But now…you know, I live in Lakeland."

> **Marilyn:** "Now have you ever lived in a camp with others for safety?"

> > **Willie:** "No, except I lived on the sidewalk at the Star of Hope, and cause the Star only had a few rooms available, I was on the sidewalk behind some guys."

> **Marilyn:** "Then they don't have any more room?"

> > **Willie:** "When it starts rainin' they open the parking lot up under the police station. Most of the time if it rainin' you have a cardboard box up over you where the rain don't get to you. But if it's cold you got to get as many blankets as you can to deal with it cause I don't get into doorways to get out of the cold cause people call the cops. You get arrested and go to jail."

> **Marilyn:** "And is it better in jail than out on the streets?"

Willie: "They got more drugs in jail than they got out here."

Marilyn: "Do you get beat up in jail?"

Wille: "OHHHHHH Yeah!" (said emphatically). "I saw one guy; he was a guy whose jaw was broken for no good reason by another guy in jail for murder. The guy told him he better not say nuthun' so the guy laid down behind the door so the guard could not see him. I went up to the guard and told them there was a guy behind the door who was hurt. The guard went and saw his jaw was broken and took him to the hospital. When I went to jail, I went to County. I got a sandwich and a dude about 21 told me "That's my sandwich." I said you did not get it and there ain't nobody gets it for you. So, I laid back down and he hit me upside the head. A guard thought we were fighting and put both of us in a room. I said that man hit me for no reason at all. Another guard said he saw the whole thing."

Marilyn: "Do you see people who are older than you being victimized a lot? "

Willie: "Yeah, there was a man older than me he was hit upside the head here one day and got his check cashed. He walked outside that door and two men robbed him. The next day, he got a check cashed and about two blocks away, he got hit upside the head and they robbed him again. You call the police, and they do not do nuthin'."

Willie: "I have a relationship with God because of the operation I went through. I had a near-death experience. My mother died when I was about five and when I was in an operation, I saw her, and she was in a field with a lot of flowers, and I ran to her. She said, "No, no, it's not your time yet." So, I stopped. But it was so peaceful and quiet there. It was wonderful. I woke up and I still felt it. I feel like if I die, I want to die in my sleep because I saw my grandmother and she was in pain, terrible pain for about a week.

I don't want to be like that. So, I asked God, when I go, I don't want to go in no car wreck, or be in no pain." (pause) "...I told the Man that I not going on the streets again. I try to rob someone or something, sell dope, or get killed. I ain't goin' out on the streets again. In prison, I would have to worry about someone beatin' up on me but at least I have a place to stay and food."

Willie: "I see a husband and wife come into the shelter and she has two kids. What kind of a life is that? They sleep under the bridge over there. I seen women come in here, leave their children here with no one to look after them, and go on a date, or to be more truthful, to make some money in prostitution. She come back 4-5 hours and the 9-month-old, three-year-old, and 6-year-old still sitting there. One day, they called CPS, and they took the children. Now I see they should have did that. If they hadn't those children been dead by now."

Marilyn: "God!"

Willie: "By my being here, I am covered by homelessness all the time. You see a lot goin' on that ...people come in here...a guy named Tim, they were goin' give him clean clothes, but he said, "no, give me my clothes back, cause they dirty and people give me money when I got dirty clothes. I can't make no money otherwise."

Willie: (pause) "Because you are homeless, you ain't got to look homeless. You got food, clean clothes can take a shower here... you don't got to be dirty."

Marilyn: "But if you are mentally ill and not taking your medication, sometimes that...(pause)...Tell me, in closing, what would you like for me to know?"

Willie: "Uh, we need more people like you that try to understand us and help. I'm glad. It is like, most people don't care, they don't care. They say I donate money to the homeless, but money doesn't help us. They need to come in and offer a job, a way out.

THINK LIKE YOUR DISCIPLINE...Critical thinking. #3
Critical thinking involves deeply analyzing a subject from the chapter. Learn to read critically. Develop some assumptions and question them. Then evaluate your position. By considering and responding to opposing viewpoints, you strengthen your understanding. You may ask each other's assumptions but don't use the same subject from the chapter. Use a class period to listen to other viewpoints.

CHAPTER FOUR

The slow slide to full homelessness.

Homeless individuals are regularly subjected to many daily injustices. Among these injustices is scorn and contempt from others. Later, I asked the mobile outreach coordinator about social service personnel's treatment of the homeless, like Willie. He spoke at length about what he had seen and what he had perceived from social service agencies' delivery of services to the homeless:

> **Mobile Outreach Coordinator:** "First, we don't have lobbying in state government to advocate for the homeless. We need advocates because the homeless keep getting shoved aside. Faith-based social services are not set up for mainstream people. They don't get jobs for them or housing. They just try to get them up on their feet. Faith-based agencies assume the homeless are going to hell because they are homeless and getting saved is everything (Sigh!) Even the Salvation Army is not set up for mainstream people. The old idea is that the Salvation Army was to take care of folks. Their new approaches are to help people to become independent, resolve their problems, and get them back into society as self-sufficient citizens.

> **Marilyn:** "What is the definition you use for homeless?"

> **Mobile Outreach Coordinator:** "...someone who is homeless or in a shelter or a place unfit for human life such as the case of an abandoned building under a bridge. Many live in a marginal situation, staying with family or friends for an indefinite time that they can stay. This includes up to people who would be homeless if they missed one paycheck." (pause)

Mobile Outreach Coordinator: "We must verify that a person to whom we offer services is homeless and it is easier to take someone from another shelter than it is to verify their identity and status if they are sleeping behind a building or under a bridge. In that case, they probably need more services than those who are already in a shelter. " (pause)

Mobile Outreach Coordinator: "because they don't want to be harboring criminals. They may have admitted a serial killer and there is liability involved without appropriate identification. If someone is killed, then they are liable. Ex-cons who have served their time are supposed to have a place to live. Our coordinator of outreach did a survey three years ago of 1730 apartment complexes and out of those, only seven would allow an ex-con to live there. Housing and job markets are limited."

DONNIE: The researcher reminded Donnie that they had met.

Marilyn: "What do you want to tell me about being in the situation you are in today?"

Donnie: "We think at times we have a lot of anger. We have a lot of anger at other people because we feel like we paid in social security and income tax. I filed for disability and was denied. It is a shame that society pushes you around because you are getting *older*. I just thank the Lord that I have the energy to push back NOW!"

By using the third person to answer, Donnie was again trying to distance himself from being like the others, e.g., homeless.

Donnie: "For close to a year I didn't have any energy to push back. Right now, I been feeling good and got energy and been thinkin' bout getting a job for a couple of years so I can make it to 62 and get my SS checks." (This is his dream.)

Marilyn: "What was your experience of going into a shelter for the first time?"

Donnie: "The first time, being an elderly white man in a 90% black environment, you get a lot of bad words, and you get pushed around a lot. They really must get to know you and find out that you will not take it before they will leave you alone." Donnie was quiet and the social worker kept writing. (he pauses, sits up straighter, and continues)

Donnie: "When someone gets pushed out, they end up real homeless. They are – literally – on the streets. At the Men's Shelter during the rain 200-300 people were pushing to get into the shelter. They push you until you leave and end up sleeping out of a cardboard box in a weed patch with a piece of plastic sheet over them. Thank the Lord I can get a little money, find a cheap hotel room, and get some peace with some real sleep. This takes the pressure off. There ain't nothing you can do. You just feel helpless."

(pause)

Donnie: "Sometimes you will go into a depression and have to be medicated…" He emphasizes "medicated." "They gave me Paxil, and I took it for a while but stopped because they referred me to a clinic on the other side of town and I could not get there for the appointments."

Marilyn: "Why in the world would they do that? "

Donnie: "The workers in the agencies and clinics are insensitive. They just want their job, and they are not thinking about their clients. They want their paycheck, and they want to look good. I listen to it all the time. It is not just my opinion. I know of two or three guys that are in their sixties – I think the most crucial time in a person's life is between sixty and sixty-two before you get a check, it is something that will get you out of the cold…get you a cubicle to be able to feel safe." (He pauses and looks sad.)

Donnie: "In the shelter I am in, even though I have to check out and, in every day, they have three meals a day and a clothes exchange…" (he laughs) "You leave your dirty, ragged clothes for another set of clean, ragged clothes."

(He laughs in a chagrined kind of way.)

Marilyn: "Do you have family around?"

Donnie: "My parents died in 1966 and my younger sister, the one I was close to died. An older sister is ten years older – they don't live in this city. I have a couple of nieces living in Pasadena. One works at Baylor. We are not close. I can call them when I am really in need. I can call my daughter who is 30 and lives in California."

(a long pause)

Donnie: "…have not seen my daughter for a lot of years. She can travel but never comes…I tell her it will be a couple of years before I can get a steady income…I will come to see my grandkids then. She does not miss me that much because she has not been with me for years. It is not like… (pause)…I can do nothing about that… can't afford to get stressed out and worried about my daughter. Her mother is going to make sure she is fine, and she is going to make sure of everything."

(He sits up straighter and moves to another subject)

Donnie: "People say why don't ya run and get you a job? I've had it, what do I that for? I have no responsibilities… but me. All I am thinking about is getting a check and retiring. And going fishing…I'm not at all worried about the rest of my life. You know? I just take it day-to-day. I never used drugs or smoked, and I don't today but I do buy things like radios, and watches. I am good at that. The Lord gives me a little gift that I learned on the farm – buying and selling things…trading…you know."

Donnie: "I am still sharp enough to make a good deal. Everybody is different. I meet a lot of people who have never had anything in their life. It is a way of life. It is the tramp trail."

Marilyn: "Can you tell me what the *tramp trail* is?"

Donnie: "What is it? This means we sink from a day center to the three shelters in Houston to the bunkhouse situation to cheap hotel rooms to cheap boarding house rooms. A lot of these guys have been on the street since childhood. I see a lot of this coming out of Ben Taub (Hospital) – they may have worked most of their lives but becoming elderly, they could not work enough to keep money coming in. They do day labor – they injure their foot or arm – for these people, they don't have any money. Once you lose that money and hospitalization from the job, they come out of Ben Taub – they end up in three shelters: Salvation Army – 8 days then pay $7 per night, or you must leave; Star of Hope Mission – go in and register for a bed – sleep – take your bag and leave – sit for hours someplace. The Open Door Mission – you can only stay 90 days – then you must do volunteer work 10 hours per week cleaning and picking up stuff. With poor health you end up being between a rock and a hard place – you end up back on the streets." (He sighs a big sigh and shakes his head.)

Donnie: "I see people stay under a bridge – pick up cans or sell newspapers, just go to one of the multiple food lines in the city. Some get in trouble…the worst thing is that they are competing with all these young people who do not work. Of course, there is a certain group of people who have mental and physical problems – alcohol and drug problems – it just takes it all away from you. I thank the Lord that I ask for strength to keep me going and that is the only way I do it. I do not need a job." (A rhetorical question, he chokes up, and looks down,)

Donnie knew he could not get a job because he did not have a home address telephone or transportation to get to the job. He lived with the fantasy that things would magically change.

Later, I made a point of finding the clinical director and asking him to check on Donnie because he was upset with the feelings coming up for him in the interview. Donnie, born into poverty, living one paycheck away from being destitute most of his life, found himself becoming more and more defenseless. He felt his only way out was reaching age 62 and claiming his social security benefits. He also appeared to be losing hope that he would somehow make it out of this conundrum that was his life. He tried especially hard to see himself as different from the others. At times though, he saw clearly his life and how it looked to others.

Billy

The director of the resource center asked a black man sitting in the lunchroom if he would consent to an interview. The man nodded and looked me up and down. After explaining about the research and offering the informed consent form to him, he was asked if he would mind being taped. He said no, very firmly. He looked angry and he demanded that I write down exactly what he said and nothing more. He had experience with things being written by researchers and clinical personnel that he did not like. Without pausing, he stated he was not homeless. He only came to the SEARCH resource center to hang out and play dominoes and cards. He lives on the southwest side of Houston and rides the bus. He gets his check from the V.A. Hospital. Without stopping, he veered off into talking about the Book of Proverbs, articulating its contents about living with the right woman. He looked suspicious and said that God made women for a man and times have changed. I wrote silently as he talked. He said a black man used to have to go to a white café and had to stand out in the back.

Billy: "I have a lot of animosity." (his words) "All I was doing was dancing to their music. One of these days this will change – we are still in bondage."

Marilyn: I continue to write, and he pauses when it is announced over the loudspeaker that the lunch line is open for two hours.

Billy: "I don't eat at SEARCH I give my plate to whoever needs it. The folks who come to this place are human. God said to help each other. "Cause you don't have what I have that don't make you less than me. No dogs come here. We be human – on the same page with God."

He then went into mumbling rather incoherently. "St. John – adultery. Moses' law. A woman should be stoned to death. Jesus – he who has no sin, throw the first stone."

Billy was an example of a mentally ill man who was not getting any better living homeless. He wanted to make sure that I, the researcher, knew he was not homeless. He wanted to be thought of as a normal man.

I waited several minutes and then went to the director's office. He knows Billy. He has been homeless for 4-5 years. He was a barber for 28 years. The director said Billy was suffering from a head injury suffered in the Vietnam War. He has good days and bad days, but the director chose him because he was less "dangerous" than many in the room. When asked what he meant, he stated many were unpredictable because of mental illnesses, they refused to take medication, and they have been known to hit, bite, yell, and kick when feeling threatened. Very emphatically, the director cautioned me that believing all homeless are crazy, drunks, or dangerous puts them on the margins of society.

The Mobile Outreach Coordinator

Homeless people suffer from various degrees of mental instability. The mobile outreach coordinator related an actual event that still outraged him. The mobile outreach van staff received a call reporting a man running down the street one cold night wearing nothing but his boxer shorts. It took them hours to persuade the man to come with them to a government hospital. He was hallucinating and covered in his feces when he was presented to the in-take person in the hospital. The woman screamed at the outreach team to get the dirty lunatic out of there, bathe him, and then they would admit him. The coordinator said to me about this incident:

"My pet peeve is seeing people falling through the cracks of the very system designed to help them. Many people don't fit into any program criteria. This case was easily remedied; we bathed him and took him back. Others must go from agency to agency, bouncing forever back and forth. They go into a kind of learned hopelessness. They have had so much experience with no one helping them that they just become, (pause…) they just get to the point where they refuse to believe that they can or will be helped."

What the coordinator was talking about with Willie was learned helplessness. He could not fight what was happening in any way except to express himself verbally. No agency is equipped to take people directly from the streets and house them immediately because of all the problems that normally must be addressed by that client. For example, with no identification, he will not be accepted at the Salvation Army, or the YMCA, or even be able to get a cheap motel room. In the city, if a motel owner is found with a homeless person living in one of his motel rooms, without an ID, the owner can be fined up to $2,500. Most shelters will not take them."

Marilyn: "So, this is very frustrating for you."

Mobile Outreach Coordinator: "You bet. I don't have as much problem with the homeless as I do when I see situations that irritate me. We will work our butts off getting someone into the program or getting them started and the people at an agency will do everything that they can to put them back on the streets. I guess they do this because they believe that these people are beyond help. Three days later we are doing the same thing again for them. Sometimes it is the homeless' fault, but I get ticked off when it is intake people in the agencies passing judgment. And that happens a lot more than agencies want to admit. Most of the time we go with them into the intake. When we first started doing that, I would catch flack for this. The intake people tell me I can go but I say that I am going to wait until I get their identification and get them registered. So, there is no reason to be booted out after I leave. This would get some intake people upset."

Robbie: The Shopping Cart Woman

We drove around the block and pulled up under the overpass. All five of us in the van got out and walked over to her. Up close the woman appeared to be about 55-60 with leathery looking very darkly tanned skin. She had multiple deep crinkles that went up and down her cheeks and her eyes were blue, clear, and intense, not mean, just intense. She had on an old T-shirt with no bra and breasts that hung at her waist. She looked like she had been on the street for years.

Mobile Outreach Coordinator: "This is Marilyn, she's riding with us. This is Robbie. I've been knowing Robbie for what, about two years?"

Robbie: "I want to show you some pictures, are you ready for this?"

She pulls out a Kodak picture pack and flips through the pictures until she finds what she wants to show him. He looks at the picture.

Mobile Outreach Coordinator: *"Hmmmmm"*, (not knowing exactly what to say.)

She stands there expectantly looking closely into his face as if anticipating a strong answer. She does not look at anyone else.

Mobile Outreach Coordinator: "This looks like your boyfriend. Where is …

Robbie: "He's in prison, but before he went, I took these. Don't you see something scary?"

Mobile Outreach Coordinator: "Hummmmmm"

Robbie: "Look at the red circle around him, and look at this, what do you see?"

She points to a couple of spots on his head on each side.

Robbie: "Can't you see them? They're horns. He is the devil. I always knew he was a devil; now I have proof he is."

She shows the picture to me, looking at me expectantly. I investigate her serious face, and I don't know what to say. In the picture, a younger man is sitting in a chair with her black dog held solidly in front of him on his lap. There is a large red/yellow circle all around him but nowhere else in the picture.

Marilyn: "There sure is a big red/yellow flash around him."

She seemed satisfied with that, and she showed me some more pictures.

Robbie: "Look at this picture; this will blow your mind."

She showed the picture to me. The same man is passed out or sleeping on a cot wearing smoke. The puffs look like little clouds. They are just around his body.

Robbie: "Ghosts!" She has tears in her eyes.

Marilyn: (reaches out and touches her arm lightly)

Mobile Outreach Coordinator: "Robbie you look scared right now." "I don't think you need to be afraid of what you see in the pictures, because he is not here, right?"

The coordinator looks at the researcher. "Are you scared Robbie?"

Robbie: "Hell yes, look, he is a devil. He hurt me and my little puppy. He choked him like this." She held her hands up like she was choking the little dog. "I put him away. I called the cops. I told him he could never come back! I ain't goin' to let the 'sum of a bitch' stay!"

Mobile Outreach Coordinator: "I'm glad. It's a good place for him to be! Bad guy, bad."

Robbie: "A devil, I tell you."

She shuffles through the pictures again.

Marilyn: "Robbie how long have you been living here in Houston?"

Robbie: "You mean, on the streets? 23 years on and off."

Marilyn: "What has the time been like for you?"

She looks intently at me and then gets close to my face, lowering her voice as if sharing a secret. Others could hear her.

Robbie: "Cool, cool. (pause) not with that sum of a bitch, though! Ya know what a 'seer' is?"

Marilyn: "You mean like a psychic?"

Robbie: "Yeah, but I am part Indian so a seer: someone who knows things, things she don't want to know sometimes!"

Marilyn: "Yes…I believe that there are people who can know things outside of our usual realm of knowing. Are you a seer?"

Robbie: "Yeah, and this is why I am afraid of him. He is the devil."

Silence for a few minutes.

Mobile Outreach Coordinator: "Robbie, you are going to be OK. We will check on you some more. Just stay away from him."

She looks up at him, relieved like a child. She nods her head up and down and says,

Robbie: "Sure, I will be seeing you next time."

We join the others in the van and drive off.

Marilyn: "How did you decide 'how' to interact with her? She likes you a lot."

Mobile Outreach Coordinator: "Well, Uh… basically… I was trying to see… where she was going with this. I did not want to support a possible delusion. One of the things I have learned in counseling that is interesting, it is OK, even if I am talking to the most free-fall schizophrenic… who is seeing visual hallucinations of the devil walking across the street, I lose all credibility if I discount that person, even though I am sure that there is not a devil walking across the street." (He laughs) "You know, I am never one hundred percent sure anyway."

He laughs heartily.

Mobile Outreach Coordinator: "She appeared to be sober. She drinks at times but is not drunk. She would be perfectly happy on an isolated ranch in Montana training dogs and horses. She does not fit in the city. But she takes better care of her dogs than herself."

Pause . . . No one says anything.

Mobile Outreach Coordinator: "She is one of those cases where a lot of people would say that she has an antisocial personality disorder."

Marilyn: "Antisocial personality? What did you see?"

Mobile Outreach Coordinator: "No, I mean by the categories in the DSM-IV, you could easily classify her as anti-social. Uhhhhh most people, by what we were looking at today would classify her as delusional."

Marilyn: "She was delusional?"

Mobile Outreach Coordinator: "She was just asking us to verify what she already knew. That is, the guy was a devil and she had to get him away from her. He has bad spirits around him; he hurts her and her dogs. She said, 'I told him he was the devil, he tried to kill my dogs and I need him gone."

Mobile Outreach Coordinator: "Why would I try to interfere with that, huh?"

He turns around and looks at me as if to punctuate the point.

> **Mobile Outreach Coordinator:** "Whatever it took her to get to that decision, (pause) it sounded like a positive decision to me. He will come back after he gets out of jail and give her the usual apology: 'Oh, Robbie, that will never happen again; things will be different. I will get you a house.'

> **Mobile Outreach Coordinator:** "I am not going to discount it because that breaks the relationship. I try very long and hard to establish trust. Once you break t(hat trust, you will never get it back. It is the relationship that I can establish that starts to make things change; they will come into the resource center, for help. The coordinator was most concerned with showing respect for Robbie to keep the relationship of care going with her. (Joan Tronto stated that the morality of what we do is in our acts. It is, however, the relationship that is moral according to the nature of the care given and received.)

We drive down the I-59 feeder, going south.

The Old Man

Riding in the mobile outreach van one day in a poor area of the city, we see an old man sitting alone on the curb of an abandoned service station/food mart. The coordinator pulls into the drive within six to eight feet of him, telling us to stay in the van, he walks casually to the man. The old man's face was a mass of deep wrinkles. The creases at the corners of his eyes suggested he had smiled a lot in his life. He was not smiling now. His weary face lit up, somewhat, as the coordinator offered him a couple of sack lunches, two bottled waters, and a cigarette. Lighting the cigarette off a match, the old man waits as the coordinator sits with him on the curb. From my vantage point, they looked like two old friends leisurely shooting the breeze. After talking for about ten minutes, the coordinator returns, and we drive off.

Mobile Outreach Coordinator: "He is waiting for his daughter; he has been waiting a week. She gets his social security check and spends it," **The Mobile Outreach Coordinator reported:** "He was released from the V.A. Hospital after prostate surgery. Their rules prevented him from waiting there for a daughter who did not come. At 84 he is dependent on his daughter, and he is sure she will come. He refused to be moved to a shelter, preferring to wait for her."

Joan Tronto (1994) argued that it is in our acts that we define moral situations. However, it is not the act that is considered moral. Most moral people would consider leaving your father to wait for days after getting out of the hospital as an amoral decision. Living in a community of others we are universally charged with an obligation and duty to treat others as we would treat ourselves. Noddings (1984) wrote that the failure to respond to the needs of another represents a failure to respond to a universal moral imperative.

THINK LIKE YOUR DISCIPLINE...Critical thinking. #4
Critical thinking involves deeply analyzing a subject from the chapter. Learn to read critically. Develop some assumptions and question them. Then evaluate your position. By considering and responding to opposing viewpoints, you strengthen your understanding. You may ask each other's assumptions but don't use the same subject from the chapter. Use a class period to listen to other viewpoints.

CHAPTER FIVE

Living Emotionally Unanchored

Interviews continue with individuals providing their histories.

Willie (Using his words)

Living Emotionally Unanchored. The slide into homelessness is slow. Born into poverty, Willie had been living on the margins of society all his life. Growing up in a time of pronounced segregation and seeing himself as uneducated, unskilled, and seizure-ridden, Willie appeared to have rejected the place society assigned for him in life. He preferred to avoid community control (i.e., sister control) and he lived around others with whom he felt equal.

Marilyn: "Have you had seizures ever since you were a child?

Willie: "No mam, just 20 years from an aneurysm.

Marilyn: "Can I ask you some questions?" What has been your experience on the streets?"

Willie: "It been up and down. When you are out there, you learn everybody out there for themselves, they got the crack and everything. When I was growing up everyone looked out for each other. But now. . . you know,

Marilyn: "Now have you ever lived in a camp with others for safety? "

Willie: "No, except I lived on the sidewalk at the Star of Hope and cause the Star only can take so many people then they don't take anymore."

Marilyn: "Then they don't have any more room?"

Willie: "When it starts rainin' they open the parking lot up under the police station. Most of the time if it rainin' you have a cardboard box up over you where the rain doesn't get to you. But if it's cold you got to get as many blankets as you can to deal with it because I don't get into doorways to get out of the cold cause people call the cops. You get arrested and go to jail."

Marilyn: "And it's not better in jail than out on the streets?"

Willie: "They got more drugs in jail than they got out here."

Marilyn: "Do you get beat up in jail?"

Willie: "OHHHHHH Yeah!" (said emphatically).

The Elderly Homeless

The elderly homeless, defined by HUD as age 50 and older, face the future with fear. As they become weaker, sicker, and more unable to protect themselves, they know they are easy prey. As a result, they either avoid all others or find a "camp" to live in with multiple others who protect in numbers. If their memories begin to fail and confusion sets in, the elderly homeless person may forget where to go for food or help, and at that point, he does not last long.

Marilyn: "But if you are mentally ill and not taking your medication, sometimes that . . .(pause)…Tell me, in closing, what would you like to tell me, what would you like for me to know?"

Willie: "Uh, we need more people like you that try to understand us and help. I'm glad. It is like, most people don't care. They don't care. They say I donate money to the homeless, but money doesn't help us. I mean, it helps some, but money makes them feel good like they doin' something. They need to come in and offer a job, a way out. Fifteen dollars could buy a loaf of bread and bologna for a lot of people."

Homeless individuals are regularly subjected to many daily injustices. Among these injustices is scorn and contempt from others. Later, I asked the mobile outreach coordinator about social service personnel's treatment of the homeless, like Willie. He spoke at length about what he had seen and what he had perceived from social service agencies' delivery of services to the homeless.

Individual homeless provide insight into their lives.

Both the coordinator and the director appeared to be seriously motivated by the need both to understand the homeless and to help them. The coordinator was concerned that there was no lobbying in state government to advocate for the homeless. Both men in their own ways stated that there were no advocates for the homeless because they, the homeless, keep getting shoved aside. Faith-based social services are not set up for mainstream people. They don't get jobs or housing. They just try to get them up on their feet. Faith-based agencies assume the homeless are going to hell because they are homeless and getting saved is everything." (Big Sigh!)

Mobile Outreach Coordinator: "Even the Salvation Army is not set up for mainstream people. The old idea is that the Salvation Army was to take care of folks. Their new approach is to help people become independent to resolve their problems and get them integrated back into society as self-sufficient citizens. You ask about my pet peeves."

Mobile Outreach Coordinator: "My next pet peeve is the lack of understanding by the public. To the public, if one is homeless or an ex-con or substance abuser or to a certain extent mentally ill, (or all the above) they are considered subhuman and they are discriminated against. Laws are in place to discriminate against the homeless. Ex-cons can never get individual government funding to help with education. Don't get me started on this one!"

Mobile Outreach Coordinator: "Even child support laws have problems. If the person gets over $10,000 behind in child support, they lose their driver's license or any state license that enables them to be able to get a job and pay child support. Drug felonies as far as public assistance, even if a person has been sober for five years, should go off their records but there are no limits. No one will hire them as they are at their station in life. One or two wrong decisions and they end up homeless."

The Mobile Outreach Coordinator was frustrated and outraged at the treatment of homeless people, whether they were men, women, children, substance abusers, mentally ill, or ex-cons.

Later, I followed up the interview with the coordinator of outreach to an interview with the clinical director of all outreaches who was located at the Resource Center:

Clinical Director

Marilyn: "What is the definition you use for homeless?"

Clinical Director: "Someone who is homeless or in a shelter or a place unfit for human life such as a case of an abandoned building under a bridge. Many live in a marginal situation, staying with family or friends for an indefinite time. This includes up to people who would be homeless if they missed one paycheck."

(pause)

Clinical Director: "We must verify that a person to whom we offer services is homeless and it is easier to take someone from another shelter than it is to verify their identity and status if they are sleeping behind a building or under a bridge somewhere. In that case, they probably need more services than those who are already in a shelter."

Billy

The director of the resource center asked a black man sitting in the lunch-room if he would consent to an interview. The man nodded and looked me up and down.

Billy, without stopping, veered off into talking about the Book of Proverbs, and articulating its contents about living with the right woman. He looked suspiciously at me and said that God made women for a man and times have changed. I wrote silently as he talked. I waited several minutes and then went to the director's office. The director chose him because he was less "dangerous" than many in the room. When asked what he meant, he stated many were unpredictable because of mental illnesses, they refused to take medication, and they have been known to hit, bite, yell, and kick when feeling threatened. Very emphatically, the director cautioned me that believing all homeless are crazy, drunks, or dangerous is giving into stereotyping. He suggested placing labels on all homeless individuals as social deviates serves to keep them on the margins of society.

All homeless are not crazy, drunks, or dangerous.

Homeless men and women suffer from various degrees of mental instability. The mobile outreach coordinator related an actual event that still outraged him. The mobile outreach van staff received a call reporting a man standing on a street corner one cold night wearing nothing but his boxer shorts. It took them hours to persuade the man to come with them to a government hospital.

"My pet peeve is seeing people falling through the cracks of the very system designed to help them. Many people don't fit into any program criteria. This case was easily remedied; we finally got him to put on some clothes and a coat. Others must go from agency to agency, bouncing forever back and forth. They go into a kind of learned hopelessness. They have had so much experience with no one helping them that they just become, (emotional pause) they just get to the point where they refuse to believe that they can or will be helped. No agency is equipped to take people directly from the streets and house them immediately because of all the problems that normally must be addressed by that client. For example, with no identification, he will not be accepted at the Salvation Army, or the YMCA, or even be able to get a cheap motel room. In the city, if a motel owner is found with a homeless person living in one of his motel rooms, without an ID, the owner can be fined up to $2,500. Most shelters will not take them."

Marilyn: "So, this is very frustrating for you."

Mobile Outreach Coordinator: "Yes. I don't have as much problem with the homeless as I do when I see situations that irritate me. We will work our butts off getting someone into the program or getting them started and the people at an agency will do everything that they can to put them back on the streets. I guess they do this because they believe that these people are beyond help. Three days later we are doing the same thing again for them. Sometimes it is the homeless' fault, but I get ticked off when it is intake people in the agencies passing judgment. And that happens a lot more than agencies want to admit. Most of the time we go with them into the intake. When we first started doing that, I would catch flack for this. The intake people tell me I can go but I say that I am going to wait until I get their identification and get them registered. So, there is no reason for them to be booted out after I leave. This would get some intake people upset."

Silence for a few minutes.

Marilyn: "How did you decide to interact with the shopping cart woman? She likes you a lot."

Mobile Outreach Coordinator: "Well, Uh... basically... I was trying to see. . . where she was going with what appeared to be a delusion. I did not want to support a possible delusion---uh--- but you know. . . being supportive of her decision that she made. I wanted to support her and not discount her. I lose all credibility if I discount that person, even though I am sure that there is not a devil walking across the street."

He laughs heartily.

Mobile Outreach Coordinator: "No, I look around and they are not there, and I am saying, OK this may not be happening. They are going to say to themself, 'I am not going to tell this idiot anymore.' Anytime I am working with someone I try very long and hard to establish trust. Once you break that trust, you will never get it back. It is the relationship that I can establish that starts to make things change; they will come into the resource center, they will go into treatment, etc. That's my job."

We drive down the I-59 feeder, going south.

More about Bill (The Orphan)

Marilyn: "I know that Bill was a mobile outreach success story. I know you got him treatment and SSI."

Mobile Outreach Coordinator: "He is a vulnerable and sensitive man. He was moved from his place in the homeless community when the city wanted the place cleaned up. The city came in with the police and moved everyone out. All his possessions were gathered up, put in the dumpster, and carted off. He was left with a sheet of plastic by a fence in a parking lot on Wayside."

Mobile Outreach Coordinator: "He said by the grace of God, that, and the people that were looking out for him, the people from the camp, the people he was staying by helped him."

Both were silent.

Later in the day with Bill.

Marilyn thought, when I see him, I am reminded that he had for a time been a concert violinist with a master's degree. I think what a waste of intellect and talent but then I thank God for the gifts given to Bill.

Marilyn: "Do you mind if I ask you some more very informal questions?"

He turned to look at me. Otherwise, he was looking straight ahead. We are sitting in the second row of seats in the outreach van. I had seen Bill before at the resource center. He wore a full, gray/black beard hanging to his chest and his glasses were one-half inch thick. He could be very close to being considered legally blind. Dressed in jeans, a SEARCH T-shirt, and new running shoes, he acted embarrassed and shy.

Marilyn: "Do you have any family down here?"

> **Bill:** "No (quickly) I have very few in Oregon. I haven't been in touch with them for years."
>
> **Bill:** "My sister said she was going to give me my mother's wedding ring. But I…"

(I interrupt again.)

Marilyn: "Oh, your mother is not alive anymore?"

> **Bill:** "Quietly. My mother has been dead most of my life." (said in a lifted lilting voice) "I was four." (said quietly). "My maiden aunt, she and my grandfather, they raised me."

(Long pause, but for once I keep my mouth shut.)

> **Bill:** "I missed my mother. We were out shopping, and she had a heart attack. They took her to the doctor's office. I could not understand why she could not come home. I said, "I will be good, I promise I will be good if she comes home. He says this rapidly, louder, with feeling. I could easily feel this experience; feeling the pain that was still there after all these years. I felt very sad for the little boy who still resided deep in this grown man.

Jurgen Habermas believed that each of us store memories in our lifeworld. It is composed of the history, the ways of perceiving and responding to the world, and the cultural beliefs and expectations of our lives. We cannot step out of it. And it cannot be discarded. It functions in the formation and stabilization of our identities. At its core is a set of basic concepts and assumptions we hold in our lives. It is from the 'little boy' that Bill remembered what happened to his mother.

Marilyn: "I am just learning about the homeless. What happens to those who are older?"

Bill: "Yeah. There was one old man that I used to stay with when I was out on the streets. Or he stayed in the camp with us. He always had sores all over his arms and I they got him a ride to go to the clinic, but he was a very timid man, and he sat all day in the clinic and never saw anyone. At 10:00 at night he was still sitting there. This old man lived in my camp with me; or I lived with him. He died of a heart attack."

Marilyn: "With you, when you were there?"

Bill: "Well, yes. He was making a homestead for himself and me. He came home from selling newspapers one evening. He wanted to lie down, and I found him lying across the bed."

(Pause) "I lay down by him and hoped that he would wake up soon. I was shocked. I did not know what I was doing." (His voice changes.)

Marilyn: "Did it kind of bring up feelings? You are shaking your head yes."

Bill: "UH… yes… That was how my grandfather died. He died of a heart attack."

(Very long pause while neither of us spoke.)

Bill: "At one time I lived with a guy who was a terrible drunk. He was drunk all the time, and he got ragged. He would tell me 'Get out of here! I don't want you staying by me anymore.'"

Marilyn: "Have you ever had problems with drinking?"

Bill: "Not really, I just drank beer. I just drank to be sociable. My only drinking problem was quitting drinking once I started."

Marilyn: "Best to just stay off it…Huh?"

Bill: "You got that right."

THINK LIKE YOUR DISCIPLINE...Critical thinking. #5

Critical thinking involves deeply analyzing a subject from the chapter. Learn to read critically. Develop some assumptions and question them. Then evaluate your position. By considering and responding to opposing viewpoints, you strengthen your understanding. You may ask each other's assumptions but don't use the same subject from the chapter. Use a class period to listen to other viewpoints.

CHAPTER SIX

Hegemony is the tyranny of the majority.

Social politics are rampant in neighborhoods. Individualistic ideologies impact the social politics of a community. In cultures supporting *individualistic ideologies,* governmental politics function primarily to keep the marketplace in proper working order. In a culture with *moralistic ideologies,* government is seen as a positive way of promoting public welfare. The moralistic culture, prevalent in New England and in the Northern Plains states such as Wisconsin and Minnesota, drives social attitudes supporting a generous public welfare program. In cultures with a *traditionalistic ideology,* the community's social politics support a paternalistic approach and elitism. In this cultural ideology, the government's principal role is to maintain elitist dominance of the existing social order and is found predominantly in the South (Everingham, 2001).

Moralistic public sectors provide more funding to nonprofit organizations distributing goods and services for the impoverished when federal budgets for social welfare are reduced. While individualistic private sectors fund non-profits when the federal budget cuts occur. In line with this logic, state and local government expenditures for human services will be higher in the Minneapolis, Minnesota area than in the Dallas, Texas area (Bielefeld & Corbin, 1996).

Community Negativity

Cultural ideologies affect welfare funding decisions as well as other community attitudes toward the intentions of people applying for welfare. These attitudes are best articulated as either "the free-rider hypothesis" or "the sucker effect."

The *free-rider hypothesis* states that under typical conditions some community members will contribute to the public good while others will free-ride. People free ride because they see an opportunity to benefit without contributing or because they perceive themselves to be of no value and therefore dispensable. The *sucker effect* occurs because an opportunity exists for a person to benefit from the contributions of others. Researchers have found people will reduce their contributions to a collective effort not because they want to free ride, but because they are afraid of others free riding (Aquino & Steisel, 1992).

When dominant others speculate about the needs and intentions of those seeking welfare assistance, the real needs of the impoverished are overshadowed by myths that lead to the abuse and neglect of the needy.

The poor have generally not had a voice in influencing policy decisions affecting the distribution of goods and services to them. Some research has found that when the poor have a voice to influence policy the result is a rise in their collective self-respect, translating to the ability to secure publicly funded jobs. Miller (2000, p. 52) found that "…reducing economic inequalities is not the answer. Having a voice to express one's real needs and to affect the implementation of goods and services to meet those needs has a positive effect on the recipients (Tronto 1994).

Social policies fall into three broad categories, the public sector, private organizations, and implicit social policy. Implicit social policy is the hardest to change because these are the taken-for-granted practices that exist as the unarticulated "ways things are done." These covert policies promote institutionalized racism, sexism, and classism (Burch, 1991) and are often driven by covert attitudes sustaining practices that separate and exclude others. These policies overtly emphasize social inclusion while tolerating covert exclusion. It has been said that whatever unites people through their identification with others like themselves, also excludes those who are not like them. Thus, excluding those designated "the others" promotes the "tyranny of the majority" (Everingham, 2001).

While the bottom line for every social policy is its effect on the welfare of human beings and how well it addresses individual needs, the foundation for social welfare policy is in its intent (Burch. 1991). When the real intent is rational, explicit, and open for all to see, social policy addresses the needs of its consumers with positive outcomes. However, when the real purpose of the policy supports a hidden agenda of the policymakers, the welfare of human beings is undermined (Burch, 1991).

Service providers hold negative views.

Social service providers are frequently characterized as victim-blamers (Tracy & Stoecker, 1995) oversimplifying their views. While many assume it is possible to reintegrate individual homeless individuals into society, present social service agencies see their clients as individuals lacking skills that would enable them to be self-supporting. These agencies operate in "paternalistic ways" which promote dependency and not autonomy. These attitudes drive the present ideology of national social politics. According to some research, governmental social welfare programs only expand to include more recipients during periods of civil unrest. They contract once stability is restored dropping recipients from welfare rolls as well as reducing the ability of homeless individuals and families to be added to public welfare (Tracy & Stoecker, 1995).

Public Rituals Degrade

Recipients of public welfare are highly stigmatized in American society. Rank (1995) found that many who are on welfare have the same negative attitudes about their fellow recipients as those attitudes held by the public. As a result, those receiving welfare try to distance themselves from others, thinking the stereotype holds for others but not for themselves. These attempts to cope with the stigma of welfare are important to the understanding of their reluctance to seek public assistance because of its association with loss of dignity (Rank, 1995).

When they do see welfare entitlements, recipients exercise their social rights and make their most pressing claims on government. If they are successful in these claims, they may enter an "unusually direct and durable relationship with the state" (Soss,1999, p. 50). However, difficult encounters in the application process are politically significant because they can dissuade citizens from claiming welfare benefits. Eligible people may be deterred if they come to believe that the application process is too arduous, degrading, and humiliating. Welfare seekers come to believe that no amount of assistance is worth these "public degradation rituals" (Everingham, 2001; Soss,1999). When welfare service providers act with perceived detached attitudes, these are taken by the consumer to be dignity-denying perceptions of them being subhuman (Soss,1999).

These restrictions have taken their place alongside dropping needy people from welfare caseloads and withdrawing Medicaid and food stamp entitlements, leaving the homeless with few options (Beatty & Haggard, 1996; Marwell & Ames,1979; Rapoport, Bernstein, & Ere, 1988).

Criminalizing the Homeless

Daily activities of homeless people eating, sleeping, and sitting in public places are considered criminal. Criminalizing the homeless is a poor public policy because it defocuses civil rights organizers and social service agencies from long-term, permanent solutions to homelessness to fighting for the rights of people who are homeless to simply exist. People whose life circumstances have no choice but to be homeless have no alternatives but to exist in the full sight of others. Punishing them for their life condition loads injustice on top of indignity (Williams, 1995).

Within many communities zoning ordinances have been passed imposing new restrictions on the homeless congregating in groups, on the operation of emergency and transitional shelters, and on the operation of soup kitchens serving the homeless (NLCHP: Recent Legal Updates, 2001). Police are instructed to arrest homeless individuals, break up their "camps", and throw away the few personal articles they have collected leaving them more destitute on the streets than they were before the police raids.

Bill, the Orphan, received this treatment. His camp was raided by the police when he was gone. They took everything to a dumpster leaving him with only a plastic sheet. His friends found him wet and cold, in the freezing rain, up against a chain link fence. He was left even more miserable than he had been.

Class action suits have been filed against cities on behalf of homeless people who had been removed by coercion and force and transported to remote locations, abandoning them (NLCHP: Recent Legal Updates, 2001). Other communities have prohibited shelters from serving meals to non-shelter residents unless the shelter obtains city authorization. These communities have also required at least one off-street parking space for every three beds provided in the shelter (NLCHP: Civil Rights Violations, 2001). When these community sanctions are enforced the constitutional rights of the homeless as citizens of the community are violated. If homeless people are singled out for punishment, experience a limiting of their rights to free speech, are punished for their involuntary behavior, or have their property seized or destroyed unreasonably, the community is participating in civil rights violations.

Discrimination occurs in rental housing due to a person's race, color, religion, sex, family status, national origin, or disability. Neighborhoods do not allow group homes for persons who are mentally ill or recovering substance abusers and homeowners' associations try to prevent the sale of property to be used as a group home or any kind of a shelter. Shelters federally funded to house homeless individuals and families arbitrarily discriminate against some homeless people turning them away for no good reason (NLCHP: Civil Rights Violations, 2001; Beatty & Haggard, 1998).

Equity is limited by policymakers.

The social conundrum of the modern era is that while those involved in policymaking generally agree social goods should be available for all, they hesitate when asked if they should be equally distributed. Equity is limited by the different social and cultural ideologies of those legislating social policy. Williams (1995) has argued citizens in a community of others have obligations to define moral, just boundaries before making policy decisions. Current social policymakers are blind to cultural differences and are unable to identify enough with individual homeless people to understand their specific needs. While this may not be intentional discrimination, it nonetheless produces a social policy representing the hegemony of dominant cultural norms. As such, injustices occur in the ways through which social goods are distributed to the poor and the impoverished (Williams, 1995). When citizens disagree about the morality of a public policy the cause is generally an inability to put themselves in the place of others and an inability to agree on what principles distinguish the conduct of their abilities to change their lives. Legislators decide which policies deserve a place on the political agenda and deny certain universal moral principles in the policy-making process (Gutmann & Thompson, 1990).

People's lives are affected.

Homeless people are separated from relationships with others, making them more vulnerable to the slide into homelessness (Luhrmann,2000). This happens as the logical outcome of their fragmented life histories. When their role models are other homeless men and women living homeless, what they learn is more dysfunction. Without a solidly experienced life history living separated from meaningful others, the person's realization of his potential is damaged. Psychological tensions resulting from being chronically separated from others are fraught with the "danger of meaninglessness exposed as the "nightmare par excellence" (Habermas, 1973, p.118). As the homeless person is chronically separated from others, he does not gain meaningful capital.

Human Capital

This capital includes assets or assigned attributes such as educational levels achieved, health status, work-related skills, and how to use normatively acceptable language. When an individual lacks these appropriate assets, this can predict life-long struggles to keep up in society (Fellin, 1998; Halter, 1995).

Social Capital

The level of social capital a person has is measured by how socially integrated one is with others. This includes a level of mutuality and trust connecting one with others.

Social Politics

These form the backgrounded context of policy debates preceding policy decision-making. Social politics are the attitudes, beliefs, and opinions of the socially, culturally, and politically dominant citizens in a society. This polity is informed by attitudes demonstrating problems of social fragmentation and exclusion rather than on social order (Hudson and Clapman, 1999; Everlngham,2001). Public policy results from the perpetual struggles by different vested interests seeking to impose their own cultural ideology overall. However, homeless people are never included in the decisions that directly affect their lives.

THINK LIKE YOUR DISCIPLINE...Critical thinking #6

Critical thinking involves deeply analyzing a subject from the chapter. Learn to read critically. Develop some assumptions and question them. Then evaluate your position. By considering and responding to opposing viewpoints, you strengthen your understanding. You may ask each other's assumptions but don't use the same subject from the chapter. Use a class period to listen to other viewpoints.

CHAPTER SEVEN

Welfare State Bureaucracies

Citizens are compensated for their role as clients of the welfare-state bureaucracies and this welfare-state compromises and pacifies class antagonism. These bureaucracies are supposed to derive their legitimation from general elections. Pacification of lower classes is achieved through the employment of democratically legitimated political power. This facilitates capitalistic existence between democracy (equal rights for all) and capitalism (Copeland & Wexler, 1985).

The limits of the state's power and ability to intervene in internal matters are clear: the social state runs up against the opposition of private investors. When there is a stagnant economy and rising unemployment, there is a reluctance to invest in those more unfortunate. The social public perceives the costs of welfare to be more costly than necessary and more affluent voters protect their standards of living during economic crises by forming a defensive block against underprivileged or excluded groups (Copeland & Wexler, 1985).

During the Reagan presidency, welfare state services were greatly reduced. The policies of his administration redistributed income to disadvantaged groups while those with more income status profited. This move by the Reagan administration resulted in a stronger separation of the federal administration from public opinion and democratic participation. The excluded and marginalized groups of society ended up having no voice in the distribution of income because they were isolated from the process of production. This policy resulted in a decisive renunciation of the welfare state leaving gaps in the state's ability to function; these gaps could be closed only through the *neglect of the impoverished* (Adler, 1991).

The ways things are done.

Of the social policies, implicit social policy is hardest to change because these are the taken-for-granted practices that exist as the unarticulated "ways things are done." These covert policies promote institutionalized racism, sexism, and classism (Burch, 1991) and are often driven by covert attitudes sustaining practices that separate and exclude others. These policies overtly emphasize social inclusion while tolerating covert exclusion. It has been said that whatever unites people through their identification with others like themselves also excludes those who are not like them. Thus, this excludes those designated "the others" and promotes the "*tyranny of the majority*" (Everingham, 2001).

While the bottom line for every social policy is its effect on the welfare of human beings and how well it addresses individual needs, the foundation for social welfare policy is in its intent. (Burch. 1991). When the real intent is rational, explicit, and open for all to see, social policy addresses the needs of its consumers with positive outcomes. However, when the real purpose of the policy supports a hidden agenda of the policymakers, the welfare of human beings is undermined (Burch, 1991).

Recently, twenty-six states have passed community ordinances limiting requests by homeless people on the streets for money, and Atlanta, Chicago, Miami, Phoenix, and Seattle have banned panhandling altogether.

*In Washington D.C., begging is now prohibited in trains, bus, and subway stations, in traffic lanes, and within 10 feet of bank machines.

*The City Council in Berkeley, California, proposed an ordinance prohibiting begging after nightfall, soliciting money from anyone who is sitting on a public bench, or putting money in a parking meter. Citizens may not be approached for a handout while using a pay phone, purchasing a newspaper, standing in a theater or restaurant line, or waiting for a bus.

*Seattle, Washington, enacted an ordinance that forbids lying or sitting down on a public sidewalk or upon a blanket, chair, stool, or another object between 7 a.m. and 9 p.m.

*San Francisco aggressively enforces anti-homeless laws. Police have started a program of taking pictures of homeless people and distributing them to liquor stores with instructions not to sell alcohol to these people or they would be fined. This practice has been abandoned.

*In Chicago, the city erected fences to close off a public area on Lower Wacker Drive. This area was a common place for homeless people to congregate and live.

*In Tucson, the city recently considered looking at a plan to privatize the downtown city streets and lease them to businesses. Additionally, the city has "zoned" homeless people by requiring a condition of being let out of jail that they agree to stay out of a two-mile square area covering most of downtown Tucson. An individual sued and the court issued a preliminary injunction prohibiting such restrictions. The restrictions have taken their place alongside *dropping* needy people from welfare caseloads and withdrawing Medicaid and food stamp entitlements, leaving the homeless with few options (Beatty & Haggard, 1996; Marwell & Ames, 1979; Rapoport, Bernstein, & Ere, 1988).

Other communities have prohibited shelters from serving meals to non-shelter residents unless the shelter obtains city authorization. Communities have also required at least one off-street parking space for every three beds provided in the shelter (NLCHP: Civil Rights Violations, 2001). When these community sanctions are enforced the constitutional rights of the homeless as citizens of the community are violated. If homeless people are singled out for punishment, experience a limiting of their rights to free speech, are punished for their involuntary behavior, or have their property seized or destroyed unreasonably, the community is participating in civil rights violations.

Toward the homeless, many in society act out of guilt, offering old clothes, food on holidays, and the occasional blanket when it is cold. Although these items are critically needed, existentially the homeless person needs more than clothes and food. They need the experience of home. Existentially, an inner sense of unheimlich, not "at home" affects them subjectively. Home is a metaphor expressing inclusion in the life of a family and a community; when one has no home, one is displaced (Hudson, 1998). Home is more than shelter. Home has deeper meaning and only begins with shelter from unkindness. It incorporates familiarity, a comfort, and a safety net shielding us from a multiplicity of assaults of the world. Home is associated with familiar security-producing cultural traditions and bonds of kinship, having more to do with our emotional needs than physical ones (Pustejovsky 2002).

Legislators decide which policies deserve a place on the political agenda and deny certain universal moral principles in the policy-making process (Gutmann & Thompson, 1990).

Benhabib (1994) stated that political agency and efficacy in the public spheres have been available only to those with social and cultural capital. She argues that all should have a voice in the pollical and economic decisions that define their lives. However, those without power and money will be systematically denuded of political agency.

Brief History of Welfare in the US since 1935

Welfare was first established during the Great Depression providing support for widows, orphans, and divorced or deserted mothers and their children. In 1935 Congress passed legislation establishing the program Aid to Dependent Children (ADC). While this was very limited in scope, support grew slowly for governmentally supported beneficence. In 1960 the name was changed to Aid for Families and Dependent Children (AFDC). The War on Poverty reduced poverty significantly during the Kennedy and Johnson administrations but ended when President Clinton signed the Personal Responsibility and Work Opportunity Act in 1996. This legislature intended to "*end welfare as we know it.*" Welfare entitlements from the government were replaced with a new block grant strategy that provided $16.5 billion per year directly to the states to use in assisting the needy. States were granted broad discretion in how to best use these funds. This legislation was born of social politics that assumed welfare recipients could find a job if they wanted one. This was one way of forcing the poor to take responsibility for their lives. It showed how little policy makers understood about the homeless. They did not have the means to know they would be dropped from receiving support, that they needed to act in advance before they were cut off (Super et al., 1996; Primus & Daugirdas,2000; Sard, 2001; McClain, 1995).

These assumptions were because the homeless were never asked whether they could get a job. If they had been asked, those developing the legislation might have heard that they could not get a job because of a lack of transportation. Also, they wouldn't be considered for a job with no home address or telephone number. The second assumption was based on an extremely naïve belief that the homeless listened to the news, knew what day it was, and would just "go out and get a job" when the welfare payments disappeared. It was obvious that the homeless never had a chance. The end of welfare as we know it was the result.

Before President Clinton's legislation to "end welfare as we know it," the only major federal legislative response to homelessness was initiated in 1983. A federal task force was created to provide information to localities on how to obtain federal surpluses for the benefit of the poor, but it did not directly address homelessness through specific programs or policies. Out of this effort, The Homeless Persons' Survival Act was developed and introduced in both houses of Congress in 1986. Only small portions were enacted into law. With this act, the Homeless Housing Act was adopted creating the Emergency Shelter Grant program and the Transitional Housing Demonstration program. President Reagan reluctantly signed into law the Urgent Relief for the Homeless Act. This act was renamed the Steward B. McKinney Homeless Assistance Act after the death of its chief Republican sponsor.

The Stewart B. McKinney Homeless Assistance Act

The McKinney Act originally consisted of fifteen programs providing a range of services to homeless people, including emergency shelter, transitional housing, job training, primary health care, education, and some permanent housing. Since its conception, the McKinney Act has been amended four times expanding the scope and strengthening the original legislation in some areas while dropping programs and decreasing funding in others. Inadequate funding has continually impeded the effectiveness of the McKinney Act since its inception. Its presently acknowledged greatest weakness is its focus on emergency measures only, responding to the *symptoms* of homelessness, not its *causes*. This focused on emergency measures instead of the causes of homelessness, i.e. low-paid work, not being paid a livable wage, inadequate benefits for those who are unable to work, lack of affordable housing, and lack of access to health care, neglecting the real needs of the homeless (NCH Fact Sheet #128, 1999; Adler, 1991; Anderson et al., 1995; Foscarinas,1996; Fuchs & McAllister, 1996).

1996 Welfare Law

Until 1996, AFDC was the principal federal-state program providing cash assistance to families with children. In 1992, the Clinton administration pledged to end welfare and required families receiving welfare to have jobs after two years. In 1994, a welfare reform proposal was introduced expanding services and requirements and was intended to increase workforce participation for single parents. It included the requirement that the parent or parents participate in a work program as a condition of receiving further assistance. The flaw with this legislation was that single parents who were required to work needed childcare as well as the other needs that originally kept them from having jobs in the first place. At this time, while the administration was Democratic, a Republican congressional majority shifted the focus of this act toward a Republican proposal ending entitlements to welfare assistance and instead, providing states with block grant. The states put the money in their bank accounts.

The 1996 Welfare Law repealed AFDC and put in its place the Temporary Assistance for Needy Families Block Grant (TANF). Under this grant, states received a lump sum of money to use for providing social welfare. Time limits, work requirements, and child support cooperation requirements were enforced for families receiving TANF assistance but did not apply to those receiving other benefits and services funded under the block grant. Each state was given broad discretion in the use of the TANF funds and the definition of the level of income level identifying "needy families." The state was not allowed to use TANF funds for any family having an adult who had received assistance for sixty months (five years). Additionally, the law set participation rate requirements limiting the welfare assistance an individual receives. An individual must be involved in one of a listed set of work-related activities for a specified number of hours each week throughout the month. This participation rate requirement could be reduced if the state's welfare recipient caseload declined. This caseload reduction credit created a strong additional incentive for caseload reduction (Greenberg, et al., 2000).

TANF Policy Implementation

Since TANF was enacted, there have been historically unprecedented declines in the state's welfare caseloads. Studies have shown that most families leaving welfare have found work, however, they have typically entered jobs paying wages below the poverty line and are unlikely to receive employer-provided health care coverage. Despite low earnings, families having left welfare were less likely to be receiving food stamp benefits or continued Medicaid coverage than those families still receiving TANF assistance. As I read and write about this, it makes me wonder how families get by without food stamps or Medicaid.

States have been hesitant to spend available TANF funds, having decided the funds should be reserved for future economic downturns. This withholding of funding, an example of implicit state policy not living up to the intent of the federal policymakers, has left social service providers struggling with demands for assistance for families continuing to face great hardships (Bond, G. et al., 1997; Pickford, 2001; Sard, 2001).

Pickford (April 19, 2001) in a Washington, D. C., press release, stated that while policymakers declared welfare reform an unqualified success, a new research report entitled, Welfare to What? reported findings of higher percentages of low-income people and former welfare recipients were still out of work and still suffering from homelessness, hunger and lack of adequate medical care. The real beneficiaries of welfare reform were state coffers and not the poorest families, reported Sue Phillips, acting Executive Director of the National Coalition for the Homeless. The TANF funds are being held in state bank accounts, growing interest instead of providing goods and services for the impoverished. The success of welfare reform, MS Phillips argued, must be measured in terms of individuals being able to obtain livable wages and address human needs. Those unable to find employment must be fed, clothed, housed, and given appropriate medical care. MS Phillips voiced the concern that the real results of the TANF legislation must be heard at the congressional level as Congress begins to revisit the welfare reform of the 1996 legislation. (Pickford, 2001; Savner, Strawn, & Greenberg, 2002).

THINK LIKE YOUR DISCIPLINE...Critical thinking. #7

Critical thinking involves deeply analyzing a subject from the chapter. Learn to read critically. Develop some assumptions and question them. Then evaluate your position. By considering and responding to opposing viewpoints, you strengthen your understanding. You may ask each other's assumptions but don't use the same subject from the chapter. Use a class period to listen to other viewpoints.

CHAPTER EIGHT

System uncouples from the lifeworld.

Society, as stated before, is conceived of as both a system and a lifeworld. The lifeworld of an individual exists as present experiences that are bound to situations" (Habermas,1987, p.128). The lifeworld exists both as the medium and the outcome of these past experiences forming a milieu from which one cannot separate oneself. This internalized milieu is related to the three ontologically formal worlds upon which subjects acting, with an orientation to mutual understanding, base their common definitions of situations.

Habermas, 1987 stated action situations, where communications occur, occupy the center of one's lifeworld and exist as the background horizon for a scene of action where individuals seek to reach understanding. Reaching an understanding, people in interaction come from a cultural tradition continually used and reused to coordinate their actions. These action situations help in forming memberships between people through the strengthening of the social integration of groups (Habermas, eds. Seidman,1989, p.173) thereby acquiring generalized capacities for action.

Structural Components of the Lifeworld

The structural components of the lifeworld provide a place where a person comes to understand the components while participating in their interactions. At the same time, these interactions confirm and renew their ideas through social memberships. Cultural reproduction of the lifeworld's connection to the new, guarantees the situations with existing conditions in the world, by securing the continuation of traditions and the knowledge needed for daily living.

Habermas suggests that individual reproduction processes can be evaluated through the responsibility of the adult personality. Disturbances occur existentially as loss of meaning: anomie (understood as loss of norms and values resulting in a sense of dislocation and alienation), and mental illness. Habermas calls these disturbances *the pathologies of bourgeois* society and suggests they can be traced back to the rationalization of the lifeworld itself (Habermas, 1987).

Action Integration and System Integration

The lifeworld first coexisted as a differentiated social system in tribal societies where society was represented as a network of communicatively mediated cooperation, binding individuals together. Societies become, for Habermas, "systemically stabilized complexes of action of socially integrated groups" (p. 188). Social integration and system integration are distinguished from one another by designating social integration as dependent on the action orientations integrated through consensus. Social integration is dependent on consensus. System integration occurs through the "non-normative steering of individual decisions not subjectively coordinated" (Habermas, 1989 ed. Seidman, p. 185). System integration does not depend on consensus. It is made by a few with the power and money to make decisions without agreement from others involved or others affected by the decisions.

A more powerful system reduces the lifeworld peripherally.

System and lifeworld are differentiated from one another through a process designed in such ways that as the complexity of the system increases, the lifeworld becomes more peripheral. In modern societies with the increased improvements in the system, the lifeworld is reduced to a subsystem. An example is that as our society has embraced the computer world with everything involved, the homeless have become peripheral because of a lack of the skills to participate fully. Simultaneously, power and money become more detached from the social structures having been set up to facilitate social coordination. The system, however, needs to be anchored in the lifeworld. With economic and bureaucratic spheres emerging to regulate social relations through money and power, the norm-conforming beliefs and attitudes of social members are made peripheral to system imperatives.

As system complexity grows exponentially through the steering mechanisms of money and power, systems get detached from social structures that are needed to promote social *integration.* Action is necessarily oriented to mutual understanding but is separated from normative contexts and interferes with the integration of society that is needed for those systems to be managed. This new level of system differentiation is now seen through a general political order that can only be absorbed into the lifeworld through the interpretation of society as a class society (Habermas, 1987).

The Uncoupling of Lifeworld and System

In modern society, the uncoupling of the system and lifeworld is experienced objectively. The social system is no longer intuitively understood through everyday communication. It has become something to be understood separately and objectively. This separation reflects a growing distance between society and the lifeworld. The system of institutions becomes dependent on legitimate orders and formal procedures needed to establish and justify socially agreed-upon norms.

What makes the uncoupling of the system from lifeworld possible is when action-oriented toward success is uncoupled from action-oriented toward understanding. Power and money become everything in place of communicative agreement. Money removes communicatively achieved agreements from the domain of economic behavior, allowing such behavior to become only action-oriented toward success. Formal power allows one with power to tell one without power what to do to achieve success without basing it on the norm first.

The ever-increasing number of individuals sliding into homelessness may be partially explained using Habermas' theory. Because the system is growing and becoming more sophisticated and complex, it is closing out the lifeworld (the individual). People who are in serious jeopardy of homelessness are sliding onto the streets and suffering from anomie and growing dislocation from the rest of society. The individual becomes more distanced from society and, therefore, peripheral, not participating with those who make decisions for others with less political power. With less ability to make decisions about their futures, they are dependent on others making the decisions for them.

Habermas (1987) strongly suggests that before those who make social policies for the institutions must be based on universal principles of what promotes a good life and on what is right for others as well as self. Having the ability to connect with larger social conditions other than self is a challenge for most people. Those not living homeless do not have the ability to imagine themselves in the situation of having no place to live or to sleep and not having anyone to help them out of their predicament. Many people do not have the ability to examine their own lives and see from the perspective of how their life could intertwine with those living homeless. It requires that they not see themselves as different and better than those living homeless. It requires that they see themselves through a lens that fosters empathy and critical thinking.

Meaning is instantiated in social action.

A person acts with the world according to his preconceived beliefs. The mentally ill man sleeping under a culvert with a robot positioned over him is an example. He believed the robot would protect him. People act with the outside world according to their preconceived notion of their place in it. The homeless man's belief in his place in the world affected his view of himself. This view, in turn, supported his daily, routine identity claims that gave him a sense of security and understanding.

Mutually shared understandings between participants in interpersonal communication situations are reached by our interpretations of the three ontological worlds. Certain patterned activity has mutual meaning for subjects in communication with one another if both participants share common cultural heritages, ethnicity, or socio-economic backgrounds. What one is familiar with becomes the standard of what is normal and is projected onto others.

As mentioned before, when a person is separated from the society of others, he is unable to cope alone. Habermas (1973) borrowed the idea from Durkheim that when an individual is isolated and alone, this individual will be unable to cope because of the psychological tensions resulting from this aloneness. Homeless people existing separated from the company of others and alienated from meaningful relationships may mentally compensate by moving into a world of disorder, senselessness, and madness. Reality and identity are transformed into an existential crisis of meaninglessness. Anomie, the alienation from social norms (the longer being homeless, the more detached one becomes) becomes unbearable for the individual.

As Mead hypothesized, the "I" is only understood within the context of a "we," and without interpersonal communication with others, the individual sinks into a world of unreality (Habermas 1984, p. 99). In this unreality, the individual no longer has a grip on the capacity to make existential decisions for self. One is unable to "discern who he is and who he would like to become" (Habermas, 1993).

THINK LIKE YOUR DISCIPLINE...Critical thinking. #8

Critical thinking involves deeply analyzing a subject from the chapter. Learn to read critically. Develop some assumptions and question them. Then evaluate your position. By considering and responding to opposing viewpoints, you strengthen your understanding. You may ask each other's assumptions but don't use the same subject from the chapter. Use a class period to listen to other viewpoints.

CHAPTER NINE

The ethic of justice informs the ethic of care.

This chapter is the sustaining foundation for this book. All findings and understandings will be addressed revolving around what is just and what is care. The term sustaining foundation emphasizes the importance of a strong base. It's about creating a perspective that is resilient and can withstand challenges over time.

The perspective of justice focuses on general, universal principles of fairness, rights, and duties, while the perspective of care focuses on personal relationships, responsibilities and obligations stemming from these relationships. Often viewed as contradictory by theorists in both perspectives, these orientations have recently been considered as both being necessary to understanding moral experience. They must work together, the universal and the 'particular. The care perspective implicates both the private as well as the public, and the justice perspective informs the practice of care, whether in the private or the public. Both are explicitly and implicitly moral, adhering to the normative notions of what is good and bad in a society, and both are articulated through a moral lens (Benhabib,1992).

The Ethic of Justice

Questions of justice arise anytime one person is treated differently from others. Justice speaks of duties and obligations as ethical goods for self and others (Benhabib,1992).

Ethics (morality) are defined as rules of conduct concerning the rightness and wrongness of actions and the goodness and badness of motives and ends. As moral conduct, the goal of ethics is to answer the existential questions of the "wherefore of our lives" (Habermas, 1993, p. 118) by exposing our daily conduct to the normative scrutiny of the expectations of what is considered good and just by a community of others.

John Rawls (1971) articulated a theory to evaluate the justice of institutions, just actions, and society. Rawls argued each person is universally entitled to have secured for them an equal right to basic liberties and economic inequalities mitigated so they are to the greatest benefit of the least advantaged and are attached to fair equality of opportunity. This abstract and universal principle is not adhered to when it comes to homeless people who have no power or money. They are discounted and do not receive the same kind of treatment as others because they lack political agency. While justice informs social behavior and exists as the highest ideal to be reached by rational society, it is, however, slightly unrealistic because in our times homeless people do not have an equal right to basic liberties.

The justice perspective is one way of seeing moral problems. Human relationships can be seen as public or private. These relationships are characterized in terms of equality and attachment, and both constitute grounds for moral concern. Elements of these moral judgments are self, others, and the relationship among them. From the justice perspective, the self is seen as a moral agent standing against a background of social relationships judging the conflicting claims of self and others against a standard of equal respect (Gilligan,1987). Potential errors occur in justice reasoning arising from the tendency to confuse one's perspective with an objective truth, i.e. being tempted to define others' perspectives in terms of putting oneself in their place. This is largely impractical because those who have never experienced homelessness have no idea of the depth of despair and anomie experienced by living homeless and having no way out. If they have lived homeless for years not experiencing the comfort of safety and care, they are existentially vacant. A homeless person then feels disconnected or adrift without a clear sense of significance in the human experience.

The Ethic of Care

The fundamental nature of caring is found in the private realm of the family but is not limited to the private. It has been considered, traditionally feminine, associated with the mother in society. A prerequisite to offering care is the ability to see another's reality as a possibility of one's own, allowing feelings to be aroused and motivating action. When one can put himself in the same situation and understand how the other feels in the same situation (position-take with the person), the other's reality becomes real. It is delimited by the moral virtues of receptivity, responsiveness, and relatedness. A moral act of caring involves care that is accomplished in real situations with individuals, not in the abstract (Noddings,1984; Held, 1995; Tronto,1994).

Early feminine theorists understood caring as both a practice and a disposition. It includes direct acts in specific contexts addressing specific needs. To offer care to another requires placing them before oneself. When this care is ethical (moral), the importance of human relationships becomes a key element of the good life (Tronto,1994; Gilligan, 1977).

Nell Noddings,1984 argued that care is conducted primarily through face-to-face encounters with a caring one and for one who is cared about. For the caring one to offer care, one must allow engrossment in the other. The one cared for must, however, accept the offer of care. Noddings, suggests "for the relationship to be properly called caring, both parties must contribute to it in characteristic ways" (1992, p.15). Noddings, argued that not caring is the opposite of securing for another "the good;" and failing to do so represents a deficit as a person. The old man on the curb waiting a week for his daughter to pick him up informs us as to the deficits of his daughter. Rational reasons must be presented for wanting to offer care and one must be able to persuade a reasonable, disinterested observer that we acted on behalf of the cared-for, thereby meeting the other morally. This "ethic of caring locates morality primarily in the pre-act consciousness of the one caring" (Noddings,1984, p. 9). Caring daughters would have this conscious attitude that requires "apprehending the other's reality, feeling what he feels as nearly as possible," and becomes the essential part of caring from the view of one caring (Noddings,1994, p. 16).

The active attempt to care for another is a normative value in Western society and as such, it is conceptualized as the interplay between an intention and an action (Held,1995). Feeling compelled to act on another's behalf (intention) is important to fueling the commitment toward acting. This is called an inner view of care. It is more than just an intention; it is that which motivates us to act in response to the perceived distress in another. As such, the response is seen as an explicit act of moral choice (Walker,1998; Habermas,1984,1987; Tronto,1984; Blum, 1994).

Lawrence Blum

The notion of caring for another as a moral act was further articulated by Lawrence Blum (1994) who emphasized care as particularistic rather than universalistic. He addressed the justice/care dichotomy saying caring cannot be guided by universalized principles but only worked out by meeting very specific needs with highly particular responses. The feelings and virtues associated with caring, involved for Blum, coherent and intelligible forms of moral motivation and understanding that cannot be founded on principles. He articulated caring as a type of moral judgment.

Seyla Benhabib

For this major theorist, justice, belonging to the public realm, exists in binary opposition to the private realm of care. Benhabib,1992 strongly argues for justice as the center of a moral theory infused within the public realm. Public space is constituted through general social norms and collective political decisions and generated by system procedures. The procedures directing the distribution of dissimilar social goods ought to be just and these goods "ought to be distributed for different reasons by different procedures and different agents derived from different understandings of the social goods" (Rawls,1971, 2001; Gregor,1996; Benhabib,1994.

Benhabib argues the justice perspective, saying that individuals living within a community of others "ought" to have the right to decide in what manner to pursue their conception of what constitutes the good life. In theory, the right to pursue these individual choices is preserved by basic liberties. These basic liberties prevent interference by those who hold different conceptions of social good. (Walker,1998; Habermas,1984; Rawls, 1971, 2001; Gregor, 1996; Benhabib,1992).

While articulating some of the problems of modernity, Benhabib's conjecture is that it is the loss of political agency and efficacy that is primary. Average individuals in society have less ability to exercise political agency and efficacy because of the increasing distance occurring between the individual (lifeworld) and the system. There is less importance placed on a sense of belonging, oneness, and solidarity resulting from the more limited opportunities to participate in the community. For those who live lives apart, consequences occur because of a decrease in political and social capital. This happens when the distribution of social goods is focused on meeting a diversity of needs, membership in groups, merit stratifications, and contributions. No longer is a single set of principles of distributive justice enough to relate to the differing concepts of the good life and differing cultural understandings among individuals (Benhabib,1994; Taylor, 1979).

The principle of public participation, (as Benhabib,1994 understands Habermas,) embraces autonomous political reasoning and discourse as central to the public sphere. Problems arise in modern societies that act to discourage public discourse. These problems include (1) access to class, race, gender, and religion, (2) money and power, (3) individual losses of agency and efficacy due to the emphasis on power and money, and (4) difficulties for individuals to develop solid conceptions of self, while existing within community settings.

Dilemmas of Modern Identity

Benhabib,1994 suggests that a just distribution of social goods ought to enhance all citizens' exercise of political agency and control to address the dilemmas of modern identity. These dilemmas include estrangement and the anomie of homelessness. Public sentiments do not encourage reconciliation and harmony. Political agency and efficacy in the public sphere have been available only to those with social and cultural capital.

Benhabib,1994 argues that all should have a voice in the economic and political decisions defining their lives. People living homeless have no voice at all in the outcomes of their lives. Those without power and money are systematically denuded of political agency. When the basic rights and liberties of those without social and cultural capital are violated, democracy is suspended. When social politics reflect concrete and universal democratic attitudes, the meaning of these basic rights, what they entitle one to, and their scope and enforcement will close the gap between those with power and money and those without. The exercising of moral judgment, however, is required by those with power and money to make policy decisions that do not subsume the politically disadvantaged under abstract principles (the homeless being forgotten during the pandemic) solely. Those with power (those dominant) should consider locating those without power so that they will receive equal liberties (Benhabib,1994).

Responsibility of Dominant Others

The *theory of discourse ethics* argues that it is the moral responsibility of dominant others to acquire more knowledge and understanding of the specific differences in other citizens' culture, structure, and history to offer equitable and rational public entitlements that meet individual needs more appropriately. (Habermas, 1987). Benhabib agrees with Habermas' discourse ethics, adding that the provision of justice can be challenged considering interpreting others' needs within an enlarged domain of moral theory. This interpretation will result in issues of justice and questions of the good life being moved to the center of discourse. Therefore, contradictions existing between the ethics of justice and rights and the ethic of care and responsibility can be articulated through moral discourse. This addresses questions of what constitutes a good life thoroughly informed by principles of justice. This understanding must incorporate important assumptions about individual needs and the sustaining of individual rights.

Responding to Rawls' distinctions between justice as the basic virtue of a social system and justice as a domain, Benhabib (1994) questions how one can defend the thesis that judgments of justice and right constitute the moral domain. Habermas, she believes, articulates the answer when he says justice is "the" social virtue and that only through practical argumentation can the fairness of moral norms and the integrity of moral values be established. This practical argumentation allows for equal participation in moral discourse.

Within individual moral autonomy is instantiated the right to challenge social dogmas and create distance from socially normative roles. However, this is not allowed for the homeless who have little political or social capital. Benhabib (1994) believes homeless individuals cannot challenge social dogma because they lack sufficient political agency. The people living homeless suffer from loss of political agency and this loss is not a consequence of the separation of the personal from the political but rather a consequence of the diminishing of possibilities for agency based on one's position in society (Benhabib,1994). It is also from the lack of esteem in which the homeless are held because of the myths that proliferate based on visible circumstances. They are forced to continue being homeless. These myths are also perpetuated by public perceptions and broader public attitudes toward poverty and social welfare.

Joan Tronto, Caring as a Social Construct

This theorist approaches an ethic of care from within a moral and political construct (Tronto, 1994). Caring as a moral construct has previously been defined by the conditions of relevance locating it within contexts with social politics defining it through private realms. Tronto defines politics as the realm of allocation of resources and public order. A community measures its ethical practices of existence and moral principles through the common ways in which citizens treat one another. A community is moral when it is composed of citizens who are motivated to conduct relationships with others based on what they have agreed is important. That is, moral principles delimit the ethical treatment of others with whom we are engaged in political power struggles and the controlling of resources.

Care for the homeless is determined by the attitudes and behaviors considered most important to citizens in a community. These attitudes and behaviors inform individual community care and are understood to be both a practice and a disposition. Engagement occurs through decisions to purposively reach out to_another. The practice of care requires assuming responsibility for another and it necessitates acting. As a practice, care has a context and a location. Tronto believes that "only when care is located in a society in which open and equal discussion can occur, where there is a consensus about some notions of need of justice, can these problems be mitigated" (1994, p. 154). As a critical standard, how well or how badly a society provides care through public entitlements to its disadvantaged citizens is a measure of how well that society can adhere to other virtues as well (Tronto, 1994).

Tronto argues one cannot understand an ethic of care until one place such an ethic in its full moral and political context. The practice of care is not articulated through a concrete set of rules or principles. When others are ignored, excluded, or politically shut out, to facilitate personal concerns, one cannot be considered moral. Tronto observes that merely making another dependent upon a relationship of care does not constitute a condition of care. It may be instead, a character-destroying relationship.

Welfare has made countless homeless people and their families totally dependent on receiving help. When that help is reduced or eliminated, they are left in an incredible dilemma. When they are forced to seek assistance, they can be treated with character-destructive attitudes. This leaves them with the dilemma of accepting negative treatment by social service personnel or finding another way to feed themselves and their families.

Power Imbalances

Tronto has problems with an ethic based solely on a justice approach because (1) it assumes more clarity of thought about others not connected to us personally, and (2) it neglects to consider moral situations as being complicated by power imbalances. These power imbalances relegate caring work disproportionately to the least well-off members of society while affording the more affluent members of society the right to use their positions of power and economic superiority to pass work off to others. Women, of course, primarily occupy these positions of marginal status in society while men occupy a central one.

Tronto suggested we do not just imagine a society where "some" occupy the powerful center and "others," are made peripheral, wanting to share in the power of those in the center. Those without power have few options, either they must persuade the powerful to allow them into the existing power circles by claiming they should be admitted because they are the same or because they are different but have something valuable to offer. She makes the point that this sameness/difference debate becomes the strategic problem of those living marginal lives. Those who live impoverished, and disadvantaged cannot effectively use this logic of sameness to persuade those with power to share it. (Tronto, 1994).

Finally, Tronto argues that the ethic of care must be kept conceptually distinct from the practice of caring. To fail to do this is to commit the "naturalistic fallacy," a long-established breach of proper ethical thinking. In this fallacy, one derives what ought to be from what is. She believes an ethic of care requires attentiveness to the concrete, ongoing process of care requiring responsibility. On the other hand, the ethic of caring is an ethical system in that it stresses values of attentiveness, responsibility, commitment to action, and commitment to responsiveness.

According to Tronto what constitutes a good moral theory may be more closely tied to peoples' ways of life than to abstract, universal standards of a set of rational principles. She says some moral questions become more important in some circumstances than in others. She admits to the proposition that universal values of an ethic of justice "might" be used to inform some degree of fairness in caring institutions and relationships (Tronto, unpublished paper, March 1991).

We react to the world according to our perceived place in it.

Experiencing the reactions of others to oneself always remains in the background of the reality of how the homeless person sees himself. Habermas (1987) suggested our sense of self is always prominently present in the setting within which our lives unfold. We are situated within this setting and cannot remove ourselves from it. Therefore, every interpretation we have of the world is an "Interpretation within the frame of what has already been interpreted, within a reality that is fundamentally and typically familiar" (Habermas, 1987, p. 133). We act with the outside world according to our preconceived notion of our place in it. Through mutually self-affirming communication with others, our identities are confirmed as well as our positions as members (or not) of social groups (Habermas, 1987).

All human relationships can be seen as both public and private and are characterized in terms of equality and attachment. As such, the act of providing care necessitates interpersonal dialogue taking place in a situated context with one needing care and another providing care. This relationship was seen as volitional and intended to specifically address another's needs through a conscious moral choice. Gilligan further articulated the self as a moral agent (from a justice perspective) as one who judges relationships of self and others against a universal standard of equal respect. She delineated the context of a caring relationship as one where the self as a moral agent responds to the perception of need in another (Gilligan,1987; Tronto,1994).

The naturalistic dimension of caring has been emphasized as an interaction facilitated through face-to-face encounters. Seen as an ethical ideal, caring is considered an ethical good existing as a condition universally sought by many to see their "ideal selves" providing care altruistically for others. The caring one, to appropriately give care, must have "moved away from" (p. 16) a self-focus to be engrossed in the other. The cared-for must accept the offered care to complete the encounter (Gilligan, 1994; Tronto, 1994).

Billy observed that the woman at Christmas brought leftovers from Christmas dinner to share with those at SEARCH. However, she threw it all together in one pot of slop. There is no doubt that she congratulated herself for being altruistic and helping the homeless with a Christmas dinner. Her self-view of her ideal self is an important factor in providing dinner for the homeless. Her personal view may have been, as Billy said, that they were dogs and just providing the food was enough, not how it was presented. Maybe she did not realize that what she was doing was degrading. It was much like social service personnel when they provided welfare funds to the homeless when they came to apply for them. The homeless people were treated disrespectfully, and it was easier for the homeless people to avoid these public degradation rituals for as long as possible until they had to make the appearance and the request.

Care ethics has been articulated through a philosophic study of morality instantiated as both reflective and normative (Walker, 1998). Morality, according to Walker, consists of both interpersonal acknowledgment and constraint. People learn to be responsible *for* things and *to* others. Morality arises between people and is informed by both self-awareness and awareness of others. Moral care is understood as mutual, i.e. shared, requiring people to reach an understanding of themselves as bearers of identities defined through normatively, society-sanctioned values. Values are instantiated as practices, not theories, and as such are informed by a sense of personal responsibility (Noddings, 1984; Gilligan, 1987; Tronto, 1994, Walker, 1998; Held, 1995; Benhabib, 1992; Blum, 1994).

Tronto (1994) argued the morality of what we do is in our acts, unlike Kant who argued, that living in a community we are universally charged, *a priori* with an obligation and duty to treat others as we would treat ourselves. Tronto posits moral situations should be defined not in terms of rights and responsibilities but in terms of relationships of care. Moral people understand a balance is required between self-care and caring for others and since moral life and social life are naturally enmeshed, moral understandings are situated within specific contexts. Within these contexts, particular identities within relationships are supported by certain agreed-upon values. Seen as virtues in the justice perspective, these values hold communities together and constitute the underpinning, the social fabric, upon which societal structures of caring are sown (Tronto, 1994; Blum, 1989; Baier, 1987; Gilligan, 1987).

The Ethic of Care

The fundamental nature of caring is found in the private realm of the family but is not limited to the private. It is delimited by its' receptivity, responsiveness, and relatedness. While caring is instantiated by a moral attitude explicating the meaning of what is good, care is accomplished in real situations, not in the abstract. Failure to respond to the needs of another represents a failure to respond to a universal moral imperative (Noddings,1984; Held1995; Tronto,1994).

The active attempt to care for another, a normative value in Western society, is conceptualized as the interplay between an intention and an action (Held, 1995). Feeling compelled to act in another's behalf (intention) is important for fueling the commitment toward action. This intention, called an inner view of care, is more than just an intention; it is that which motivates us to act in response to our perceived distress in another. As such, it is seen as an explicit act of moral choice (Walker, 1998; Habermas, 1984,1987; Tronto, 1994; Blum, 1994).

The Ethic of Justice

Questions of justice arise anytime one person is treated differently from another. The ethic of justice is understood in early feminist theory as the antithesis of the ethic of care. As such, justice has been considered male and abstract, instantiated through universal principles within a public arena. The idea of justice speaks to the duties and obligations positioned as ethical goods for self and others (Benhabib,1992; Blum, 1994: Gilligan, 987). Ethical goods are moral duties among other things, composed of acting respectfully while supporting another's bid for autonomy. Blum argued these duties involve moral agency and moral responsiveness (Blum, 1994). The moral agent has an obligation and duty to perceive and respond to the needs of "the other" by answering this moral imperative positively (Held, 1995; Blum, 1994).

Justice belongs to the public realm and exists in binary opposition to the private realm of care (Rawls,1971; Benhabib, 1992). Different understandings of justice should precede those of the good life. Citizens ought to have the right to decide in what manner to pursue their conception of a good life. These decisions are preserved by basic liberties preventing interference by those holding different conceptions of the social good (Walker, 1998; Habermas, 1984; Rawls, 1971; Benhabib, 1992). A single set of principles related to the distribution of different social goods ought to be accomplished based on different needs, membership, merit, and contribution (Taylor, 1979; Benhabib, 1994). The principle of public participation extends to the centrality of autonomous political reason and discourse within the public sphere (Habermas, 1993).

Benhabib (1992) suggests distribution of social goods in a just manner should enhance all citizens' exercise of political agency and control. However, participation is not an answer to the dilemmas of modern identity: estrangement, anomie, and homelessness. All should have a voice in the economic and political decisions defining their lives. She argues moral judgment is required by those citizens with power and money and this judgment must be placed in the universal context in such a way that it comes to bear upon the particular.

Benhabib (1994) uses the arguments of Kant's moral point of view, Rawls' original position, and Habermas' ideal speech situation to question universalist legislative reason. She suggests from the moral point of view, individuals reach a stage of reasoning where they begin to question the social validity of norms and normative institutional arrangements from the standpoint of standards of justice, fairness, and impartiality. Here individuals and communities move beyond the "should" of a conventional understanding of an ethical life to a position of questioning the social validity of the moral "ought" (Habermas, 1993; Rawls, 2001; Benhabib, 1992).

Giddens (1979) emphasized that "characteristics of the social whole are separate from those of individual agents" (p. 50). He considered society and the individual to be connected in that "every person is born into an already constituted society, and every person is only one individual in a system of association involving many others" (p. 50). Within this association one must always act responsibly as well as virtuously, treating others as ends and never as means and respecting the autonomy and dignity of all people equally. For Kant, these ends exist *a priori* as duties and are expressed in such a way as to compel society to adopt them (Habermas, 1993).

One's first duty is to the cultivation of one's conscience and this duty exists as an obligation begging active benevolence through the adoption of the other's ends as our own. Citizens in a just society are allowed to act benevolently toward us only on the condition that we act equally benevolently toward others. Articulated as a universal principle, in the practice this benevolent attitude is limited to an individual's own family, neighborhood, ethnicity, or religious community (Blum, 1994; Held, 1995; Tronto, 1994). (4503)

THINK LIKE YOUR DISCIPLINE...Critical thinking. #9
Critical thinking involves deeply analyzing a subject from the chapter. In this chapter, please analyze each of the three theorists using one of their ideas for each. Learn to read critically. Develop some assumptions and question them. Then evaluate your position. By considering and responding to opposing viewpoints, you strengthen your understanding. You may ask each other's assumptions but don't use the same subject from the chapter. You may need two class periods to cover each students' viewpoints.

CHAPTER TEN

Before and after COVID-19 pandemic.

Families leaving welfare do not fare better than being on welfare. Often, they do not access government programs for which they are eligible, such as food stamps. More families report an inability to feed their children or themselves. With the reductions in welfare caseloads, many more families and individuals leave the welfare rolls. Those who went to work at some point in their first year of assistance made only about half of the year's earnings. Most are working only 30 hours a week with no paid insurance, no vacation or sick time. Overall, significant numbers of untreated medical needs (Pickford, 2001).

Private Lives in Public Spaces

Homeless people living in congregate shelter settings had trouble complying with COVID-19 safety measures. Lack of access to showers made it difficult for those living there to engage in basic hygiene like handwashing. When they were all together staying six feet away was made unnecessary because they all shared cigarettes and food. There was general disbelief in their risk for COVID-19 as they were always touching each other. They just did not pay any attention to it. Many had fears of being confined or separated from their friends. There was no rule book. They could not see their therapists so got no treatment. Staff levels and volunteers declined. (Rodriguez, 2021)

People living homeless are situated in public contexts. When the pandemic struck, homeless people were not included in the plans by the federal government or towns and cities. The US was simply not prepared to care for the homeless. Tronto would consider this a supreme failure to respond to the needs of another and home" living in a homeless encampment. Fear of getting sick, getting sick with no cell phones or ways of charging them made them incredibly vulnerable. The homeless were quickly forgotten. They did not receive in the initial days of the illness appropriate care or sometimes, any care.

Housing was always an issue and became even more critical. There is a strong correlation between health and housing. Not having a place to live was the cause of many deaths. No one seems to know how many homeless individuals died in this country due to the pandemic. Because the homeless were not included in the conversations before the pandemic, they were not included during and after the pandemic. They are vulnerable members of the community, and the community has a moral obligation to include them in crisis management plans. For a major theorist, Selya Benhabib, justice, belonging to the public realm, exists in binary opposition to the private realm of care.

The public realm is both abstract and non-particular (individual) and generally informed by universal principles. Giving care to those living without a domicile must qualify as just care that is instantiated with justice and existing as a private conception of caring. This manner of caring emphasizes society's moral responsibility and obligation to attend to the significant needs of individual people in face-to-face encounters.

Excerpts from the homeless individuals interviewed are shown positioned against existing federal laws directly affecting their lives. How states interpret these laws, and how the local policies and ordinances rising from these interpretations affect their lives, is demonstrated. While building toward a moral theory of just care, the prevailing cultural ideologies driving the person living homeless must be placed at the center of shared decision-making, affording them an equal voice in the decisions involving them.

Homeless people living in congregate shelters had trouble complying with COVID-19 safety measures. The lack of showers, sharing cigarettes and food prevented staying away from each other with six feet in between.

They simply did not believe they were at risk for COVID-19. They were always touching each other. Many had fears of being confined or separated from their friends. There was no rule book, no way of measuring their lives.

The prevailing Republican and Democratic social politics affect the manner and the extent to which services are made available to the homeless. The irony of existing social politics in most of the United States is that regardless of the political philosophy behind these politics, social inclusion is emphasized as the universal moral choice, while exclusion is tolerated.

Since people living homeless are situated in public contexts, when the pandemic struck homeless people were not included in any contingency plans. The U.S. was simply not prepared to care for the homeless. For the treatment of the homeless population to be regarded as appropriately moral, public policy decisions must meet standards of justice and fairness. Homeless people, men, women, and children were denied the ability to get and hold a place to live during the COVID-19 outbreak. Many died.

Federal lawmakers have sought to remedy the dignity-denying life conditions of the impoverished by proposing and passing federal legislation conceptualized to ameliorate their real problems. Federal lawmakers consider the plight of homeless people by objectifying and categorizing them into an all-encompassing group labeled "the homeless." By distancing themselves physically as well as subjectively from the daily realities of individual homeless people, lawmakers are precluded from understanding how they were affected by the pandemic.

The intent of the welfare law.

The intent of the welfare law was somewhat lost in its application. While lawmakers seemed to abstractly believe that homeless people are ethically entitled to the same rights and duties as all other citizens, in practice they tolerated inequity.

Donnie (The Gentleman)

This quiet man made a point of getting a haircut, when needed and wearing a shirt that, while somewhat wrinkled, was clean. He frequently expressed his frustration with shelter personnel who allowed weaker individuals to be roughed up and pushed out of long lines waiting to get a bed in the shelter. The stronger and younger men got their beds through force. Donnie was approaching 55-60 and experienced more anxiety attacks and more depression as he grew older and more powerless:

> "They push you until you leave and end up sleeping,
> out of a cardboard box in a weed patch with a piece
> of plastic sheet over you."

Donnie was reacting to the world according to his perceived place in it (Tronto,1994).

Conceived to address the needs of people like Donnie, the McKinney Act has been amended four times, each time reducing the funding for shelters for the homeless. Even emergency housing had been reduced to a bare minimum, leaving many homeless people without a place and a bed to escape to during bad weather.

This situation concerning Donnie occurred because shelters set their own rules that were generally not coordinated with other homeless services offered in the community. To have a bed for the night these men had to stand in line to register for a shelter bed by the middle of the afternoon. They were expected to find work, but these rules limited their ability to stand in line early enough to cut a bed. They had to decide whether a job was more important than a bed. If they get a bed, they must be up and gone by 7:00 the next morning, take their belongings with them, and repeat the whole process over again early in the afternoon. Having funded shelters meets the critical needs of many homeless but there simply are not enough shelters to provide for all the homeless people who seek a bed.

Benhabib (1992) argues with the theory of discourse ethics that it is the moral responsibility of dominant others to acquire more knowledge and understanding of the real-life problems of the person who is living homeless to offer them rational public entitlements to meet their needs more appropriately during a health crisis like the COVID-19 pandemic. It has been recognized that people who live without domiciles are not understood by those who write and pass policies affecting their lives. These bureaucrats have no conception of what the homeless people's life challenges are daily.

There was very little understanding of how the homeless people were suffering during the pandemic. Social services personnel understood but were for the most part needing services for themselves. As Benhabib stated, when articulated through a moral lens, questions of justice arise anytime a person is treated differently from others. Benhabib asserted that this speaks of duties and obligations as ethical goods for self and others. (Benhabib1992).

Willie

Working in the SEARCH kitchen, also included a bed for the night at the center. In our interview, he was able to communicate how he worried about not working there and not having a decent place to sleep:

> "It is brought on mostly by stress. I had a seizure about a week ago. You can only live here so long, and I was wondering, where I was going to go after this. That night I went to bed,thinking about that and the next morning I had a seizure so."

Without shelter, those without domiciles died at alarming rates. This occurred during the COVID-19 collapse of the safety net that in normal times addressed the mix of trauma, medical conditions, and addiction that accompanied homelessness even in the best of times.

When the McKinney Act became law, it was only for emergency measures and did not address the causes of homelessness. For Willie the prospect of not working at the center and not having a bed haunted him. Many other homeless men who were interviewed expressed a desire for a job. However, they did not have jobs available to them within walking distance and they did not have transportation to get to jobs at a distance. Legislators writing the welfare law were unable to understand the multiple problems that infiltrated COVID-19 homelessness i.e. low-paid work that could not support even subsidized federal housing, inadequate benefits for those unable to work, and no way to get to work.

Caring Enough

Joan Tronto, (1992) wrote that caring for people needing help in society requires that we defocus from ourselves and focus on what they need. They could not shelter at home; they had no cell phone or way to charge it. They suffered. Hopefully, many lessons were learned that will be used when the next pandemic crisis appears.

Willie and Donnie's predicaments were underscored by the coordinator of the mobile outreach team. He stated not only are there not enough services, but no one advocates for those living homeless in the state legislature. The problem with these rules is when one has no job, no transportation, no health care, no family, "no...nuthin'…" one has no alternative but to remain on the streets.

Ending welfare as we know it.

The 1996 welfare law was conceived as the solution to "ending welfare as we know it." This law has conceivably made the situation worse for homeless individuals. While there has been a sharp decline in welfare caseloads due to tough state policies enacted, it has not been due to economic good times and the decreasing unemployment rate. The welfare caseloads have been reduced as states vie for the financial incentives provided by the new law. These reduced caseloads have been publicized as proof that the new law works. The reality is that states have been dropping needy individuals from caseloads for small violations of rules, requiring them to go to work immediately, even though most cannot find jobs. When they do find jobs, the pay is minimum wage with no benefits and is not even enough to pay for federally funded housing. The states with the toughest policies have disqualified recipients after their first infraction of the rules. These states report caseloads reduced by 41.8 percent.

Perhaps the most shameful response of the states is with the broad discretion given to them as to how and when they disburse the federal funds. Much of the money is still sitting in state bank accounts gaining interest while social service agencies are struggling to provide for the homeless.

The SEARCH mobile outreach coordinator addressed this problem:

"…there are not enough areas served."

"Many people don't fit into any program criteria."

"No agency is equipped to take people directly, from
the streets, housing them immediately because of all
the problems…with no identification he will not be…
able to get into a cheap hotel."

There are not enough services for pregnant women, women with children, ex-cons who cannot get jobs or housing, substance abusers who cannot get treatment, and most devastatingly, the mentally ill who have so many problems that many social service personnel do not want to deal with them.

The test for good welfare reform.

The test for good welfare reform is whether it does what it was intended to do. In this case, if… the new law promotes working, provides housing, and meets the needs of those it was intended to help it is a good law. The 1996 Welfare law wiped away all federal requirements, imposed a five-year time limit on receiving federal money, and legislated changes in a welfare entitlement atmosphere where fraud and laziness had been rewarded. The states that have not participated in punitive measures but instead have pursued intelligent, thoughtful policies, are not rewarded. They are thought to be going against the grain. There is no question that the social politics surrounding the 1996 Welfare Law vary with the cultural expectations of different regions of the county.

Because individuals living homeless are not able to keep pace with normative standards of success, they are viewed with disdain. The views and attitudes of citizens of a community are referred to as the politics of the community. These politics lean toward securing social order rather than guaranteeing social justice and arise from the prevailing cultural ideologies in a region. In Houston, the cultural ideology is traditionalistic and supports a paternalistic approach to the poor and homeless. In a traditionalistic culture, the government tends to be a conservative one and its principal role is to maintain elitist dominance of the existing social order.

> **Willie:** "She don't appreciate the life I am living…but like I told her, I'm 58, I don't have no education, I have seizures, and I can't work like others."

> > **The Clinical Director of SEARCH Resource Center stated:** "To the public, if one is homeless or an ex-con or substance abuser or to a certain extent mentally ill (or all the above) they are considered subhuman and are discriminated against."

> **Donnie stated:** "These folks …are insensitive.*"*

Traditional, state-centered welfare has failed to prevent social problems and has perpetuated dependency rather than re-engagement in work and with the community.

In cities with an admitted lack of shelters and few jobs paying a living wage, people who are homeless are discriminated against. Local communities all over the country have passed ordinances that in effect criminalize homeless people. Social politics drive blatant discrimination through city ordinances designed for the benefit of dominant others. In Houston, few formal ordinances exist on paper but discrimination by law enforcement agencies violates the civil rights of these impoverished citizens.

Bill described the common practice of the police indiscriminately breaking up "camps" of homeless people:

> **Marilyn:** "So, what was the hardest time for you when you were living in the camp?"
>
> **Bill:** "Oh, it was the winter of 1996. The cops come along and rousted us out of the camp, cleaned it out and we had noplace to go."
>
> **Marilyn:** "They just showed up."
>
> **Bill:** "Yeah, the city made them clean up the place and we had to move. Where I moved to was by a fence in a parking lot on Wayside Drive. I did not have much protection, just a piece of plastic. With the rain and wind and cold, my clothes got wet, and it was cold."

What Bill did not say in the interview, but I found out later was the police destroyed all their possessions, leaving them more destitute than ever.

In another conversation I had with the ex-mayor of a small town close to the one I live in, who happened to be my eye doctor, proudly stated,

> **Mayor:** "We don't have any homeless in Rosenberg. What I mean is we pick them up and take them out someplace but get them out of the city."

This man appeared to be kind and caring in the office, however, what he exposed to me were highly conservative social politics that appeared to consider the presence of homeless people in their small, and not particularly nice town, as something to be ashamed. They had much more to be ashamed of in their treatment of the people they dumped out someplace in the country. The criminalization of the homeless is a poor public policy.

Joan Tronto
Care informed by justice.

The act of caring for homeless people in our communities requires us to care on a deeper level about them welfare and position-take with them in their circumstances. Taking a position with the other is required before one can even begin to understand the depth of their need or decide to act.

Embedded in an offer to care is the attitude that the one in need is cared about enough for the one caring to act.

Joan Tronto conceptualizes care as both a disposition and a practice involving taking the concerns and needs of the other as the basis for action. She argues for rethinking our conception of humans as being either autonomous or dependent. Humans are interdependent with one another. When we "take care of" another we assume agency and responsibility in the caring process. "Caregiving," however, involves directly meeting another's needs. When we "take care of" a homeless person, we give them money on the street, or we give them coats and sweaters against the cold. When the mobile outreach team meets them on the street to listen to them and offer solutions, they are "caregiving." When the outreach team drove up to the boarded-up service station to talk with the old man sitting on the curb, they were caregiving, acting out of compassion for this old man abandoned by his daughter.

To see another's reality, we must have something that disturbs our sense of fairness. Compassion arises out of being disturbed by what we see. One seeking to give care must be guided by the necessary moral insight required to make rational decisions. Willie knew when others did not care about him. When they donated money, Willie felt they did it because it made *them* feel better. While he agreed that money helped, offering a job, and a way out was the kind of care he needed.

The coordinator of the outreach team told me he was deeply saddened that helpless homeless people go from agency to agency bouncing forever back and forth in a futile search for care. Over time they have had so much experience with no one helping them that they just get to the point where they refuse to believe that they can or will be helped.

Caring for others using a moral and a political construct.

The practice of care describes qualities necessary for democratic citizens to live together in a pluralistic society. The fact that all humans need care has been difficult for liberal political and moral thinkers because the liberal framework only allows for dichotomous choices of autonomy or dependence. There is nothing in between. Social service agencies and many faith-based programs are set up to provide for the homeless. In the process of offering care, sometimes individuals appear to delight in "jacking the person without power around." When one is dependent on a relationship of care, this dependency does not automatically assure that the other is giving care.

THINK LIKE YOUR DISCIPLINE...Critical thinking. #10
Critical thinking involves deeply analyzing a subject from the chapter. Learn to read critically. Develop some assumptions and question them. Then evaluate your position. By considering and responding to opposing viewpoints, you strengthen your understanding. You may ask each other's assumptions but don't use the same subject from the chapter. Use a class period to listen to other viewpoints.

CHAPTER ELEVEN

Politics have become the means to moral ends.

Political theorists consider dependence to be character-destroying because when one is dependent, one is without autonomy. Dependence on the paternalism of social welfare, sometimes, results in homeless people losing the ability to make judgments for themselves, ending up at the mercy of others.

From Willie's point of view, he was being passed from one bureaucrat to another, each one too lazy or unconnected to go the extra mile to help solve his problem. Since Willie is a mild-mannered person, I can guess that he was easy to put off. Only if caring for others takes place in the context of a democratic social order can human dependence be recognized as a necessity that can be overcome. That is if homeless people can be given care in a manner that allows for their active participation in the process, they can learn to overcome their dependence and take over control of their lives in a manner sufficient to leave their homeless condition. Joan Tronto asserts that some in our society must work so others achieve autonomy and independence. This, however, is obscured by the separation of public and private lives and how care is distributed.

The political ideal of care states that life is delineated into public and private affairs. The public is where the ethic of justice resides. Jobs are here. The normative expectation in our society is that adults work hard *because* they are adults and ready and able to work. Most have additional reasons for being blocked in their efforts to get a job that only begin with not having a home address and a telephone, to say nothing of appropriate job skills.

Moral care

An ethic of care in the private arena (or moral caring) has previously been seen to be in a dichotomous relationship with an ethic of justice. When caring for others, whether in our families or perhaps for homeless people, comes as the result of our own experience being cared for as a child. This is where we learn to care. Therefore, the care that we may consider offering to the homeless person must be informed by our own previously internalized notion of what is just for another.

Interpersonally, the practice of caring for another must consist of deeply held personal values regarding what is just. These values must exist at the very foundations of a public policy that is aimed at providing care for impoverished others by preparing them for a more autonomous life off the streets. Joan Tronto argues this kind of care would facilitate our becoming better citizens in a democracy. When we reach out to homeless people and offer them training in life skills, budgeting, job skills, etc., the homeless person will be enabled to exist more interdependently with others in society rather than continuously following the vicious cycle of dependency.

Power Differentials in Public Care

Caring for others has moved from the private to the public through interventions facilitated by governmental laws and policies. Public welfare is public care following private notions of what constitutes care. Caring for another includes and requires a face-to-face dialogue with the one needing care to appropriately meet their needs. This kind of caring requires not only the permission of the one needing care but also their active participation in receiving the care.

Caring adequately for needy others within the public realm assumes a political position when it is based on the disclosure of how current social service agencies embody and wield power over the powerless homeless. Power differentials inherently exist between personnel in social agencies and homeless individuals. Many people holding "front-line jobs" in agencies are minimum wage earners who may have experienced a lack of power themselves. It is not hard to imagine these partially disempowered people choosing to hold the small power they have in their present job over those who have no power. It is not so much that existing rules and regulations must be changed (which they must) but that agencies must train employees to serve others better both materially and existentially. Seyla Benhabib suggests that all should have a voice in the economic and political decisions defining their lives. This *care conduct* must emanate from a new paradigm of focusing more on empowering people who are homeless by using dignity-supporting attitudes.

Care conduct in the public realm is not only political but moral as well. Moral principles support the just treatment of others, while the politics of welfare distribution involve power struggles and the control of resources. Politics has become a means of achieving moral ends through the facilitation of law and public policies.

Seyla Benhabib

Universalistic Moral Theory

Benhabib has sought to develop a universalistic moral theory. This theory defines the moral point of view within universal principles. What is *just* is defined through that which is abstract and universal, applying to all citizens equally within a public discourse. Everyone is a moral person with the same universal rights. This moral person, as the generalized (the universal) other, is capable of reasoning and acting with a sense of justice, forming a vision of the good, and engaging in the pursuit of the good. The concrete other (the particular) challenges us to view every moral person as a unique individual with a specific life history, a particular disposition, and certain endowments.

Delineating a moral point of view is not possible without considering the view of the generalized other. Universal principles of justice *must* inform the attitudes, behavior, and decision-making of those with the power to grant or deny care to the homeless. Just care is not possible without the firmly ensconced moral convictions that delimit what is just in the treatment of those without power.

Benhabib suggests that problems in modernity exist less in the loss of a sense of belonging, oneness, and solidarity and more in the sense of a loss of political agency and efficacy. This loss of political agency for Willie was a consequence of his social position as a person living homeless. He had no power to control the decisions of agency personnel regarding his requests and he knew it.

A conception of universal moral theory, restricting one to the point of view of the concrete other would be racist or discriminatory. Because concrete identities of people living homeless are constructed through categories implying a lack of control, homeless men and women like Willie are subjected to overt and covert racism no matter what the race of those who are assigned to help him. Social service personnel of the same race as the person living homeless can be biased and discriminatory. They are as contemptuous of homeless people as are others.

Billy, a man living homeless with brain injuries, spoke passionately about his value as a human being. He appeared to be very defensive and defiant regarding his homelessness and the treatment he has received from society all his life as a black man:

> "Cause you don't have what I have that don't make you less than me. No dogs come here. We be human – on the same page with God."

He struggled to maintain a sense of dignity and value in himself. However, it appeared that when confronted with a person who was trying to treat him with the respect and the dignity he deserved as a human being, he became very suspicious.

To maintain dignity many homeless individuals, use methods to distance themselves from social criticism. Some try to speak or dress like they are not homeless or refer to themselves in ways that disavow their homeless state. Donnie always had a haircut, and his beard was trimmed. Billy asserted that he was not like everyone else in the resource center waiting for lunch. He stated he lived in "southwest" Houston not in the ghetto and rode a bus to the center every day to play checkers and talk.

Benhabib states that not being aware of the "otherness of the other", e.g. Willie, all of society's prejudices, misunderstandings, and hostilities will remain just where they are: hidden behind Rawls' "veil of ignorance." She believes that Rawls' use of the veil of ignorance is internally inconsistent with the notion of taking the position of the other. By contrast, she believes that only a moral dialogue that is truly open can lead to a mutual understanding of otherness. This theorist believes that with modern society undergoing tremendous transformations, an ethic of justice is needed to occupy the center of moral theory more solidly.

Benhabib posits that when democratic politics are in full session, debates occur about the meaning of basic rights and what they do or do not entitle us. When basic rights and liberties are violated then democracy is suspended. Welfare state societies (those societies that provide welfare entitlements) are the ones in which provision becomes public by promoting a most effective patriarchal-capitalistic-disciplinary bureaucracy. In this political milieu of entitlements, individuals are subsumed under the rules of the system. In a capitalistic system, the deserving poor are provided for and those deemed undeserving are sanctioned. Benhabib considers the deserving poor to be those homeless whose poverty is not attributed to personal behavior, and they are considered deserving of care and assistance. Their circumstances result from systemic factors beyond their control. On the other hand, the undeserving poor are those who do not want to work and have individual shortcomings that contribute to their poverty. Thus, positioning them in a place where they are not deserving of care and assistance.

A Moral Point of View:

A moral point of view is not primarily construed as hypothetically carried out by an individual moral agent. It is an actual dialogue situation where moral agents and questions of the *good life* occupy center stage within this communicative setting.

The Moral "Ought" and Social Acceptability Question

When moral agents begin to move away from the conventional understanding of what constitutes an ethical life and question the distinctions between "the moral ought" and social acceptability. Benhabib questions under what conditions we can say general rules of action are valid, not simply because it is what we have been brought up to believe but because the rules are fair, just, impartial, and in the mutual interests of all. She suggests that a disjunction emerges here between the social validity of norms and normative institutional arrangements.

The effect of the 1996 Welfare Law on the specific, poignant lives of the poor and homeless violated moral ought. This law allows states the right to make arbitrary decisions about the needs of the homeless and the poor, and while remaining at a distance from the recipients. This challenges the moral ought. It also continues making assumptions about generalized others without face-to-face dialogue with the intended recipients appears to be violating the moral ought. Reducing food stamp benefits from the current level of 80 cents per person per meal to 66 cents per person per meal straddles the line separating what is just and moral from being insensitive to the needs of the working poor, the elderly, the homeless, and the disabled. This poorly conceived law does not help most of the disadvantaged precisely because it is not based on a moral point of view that illuminates its' effects on individuals living in poverty and homelessness. Fourteen cents may not sound like much to a bureaucrat, but it is to the poor. It is hard to imagine what the actual conditions are that homeless human beings live in without standing in the context of their lives and listening to the actual day-to-day struggles. They are *powerless in every way* to facilitate their rescue, and once caught in the downward spiral of the streets, they need assistance from others to get out. Universal principles of justice need to infiltrate the thinking of those in institutions charged with giving care to the people living homeless because as Benhabib argues, what is *just* becomes the center of what is moral.

Benhabib articulates an attitude of support when individuals are living within a community of others, that person ought to have the right to decide in what manner to pursue their conception of what constitutes the good life. For Benhabib and Habermas, the concept of justice and care is seen through the uncoupling of the system and the lifeworld.

Uncoupling of the System from the Lifeworld

The lifeworld of a homeless person may be filled with fear from previous childhood and adult experiences which have prompted his homelessness and from which he still suffers. Donnie mentioned the following:

> "Of course, there is a certain group of people who have mental,and physical problems – alcohol and drug problems – it just takes it all away from you. I thank the Lord that I ask for strength, to keep me going and that is the only way I make it."

I believe Donnie was referring to himself and the problems that he has experienced in life that prevented him from living a normal life. He grew up in real poverty. He has never been able to shake the notion that he was a poor man with no prospects. Alcohol and drug addiction medicated not only his fears but medicated his anxiety and restlessness. All this was stored in the milieu of his lifeworld and constantly infected and re-infected his attempts to live a normal life.

Billy, in the resource center, stated (using his words and grammar):

> "I have a lot of animosity. All I was doing was dancing to themmusic. One of these days this will change – we are still in bondage."

While Billy had suffered from mild brain injury, buried in his lifeworld was a past inundated with situations where he felt he had to bend and scrape to white men and women. He still felt he was in bondage and this view of himself in the world prevented him from seeing himself as a person of worth.

Robbie (The shopping cart) woman continued to see herself as a victim needing, to be protected both from her boyfriend and by her boyfriend.

> **Robbie:** "Yeh, but I am part Indian, so I am a seer, someone who knows. things, things she doesn't want to know sometimes." "I know things about him, and this is why I am afraid of him. He is the devil. He had my puppy like this."

Having lived on the street for 23 years, as the coordinator told me later, she had a mother who was homeless most of the time Robbie was growing up.

These people, living homeless, acted from the stored knowledge of experience, understanding the world through the knowledge gained from other experiences already internalized. Robbie interacted with the world through the personnel and the services of the welfare system.

The system, over the last 23 years, has become progressively more complex reducing the lifeworld to a subsystem. That is to say that with the complexity of the system, people like Robbie are less and less considered to be integral to society. At the same time, steering mechanisms such as power and money become more detached from social structures set up to facilitate social coordination. Because Robbie had no power and no money, her worth to society became less and less. The non-conforming beliefs and attitudes of social members become only peripherally important to the system. Habermas suggested that as the system complexity grows exponentially through the steering mechanisms of money and power, the systems get detached from social structures that are needed to promote social integration.

The great institutions providing welfare entitlements for the people living homeless have separated themselves more and more from the people they are set up in the first place to help.

As the welfare system is formed and reformed, the political entities with the power and money to alter policy do so from a distance and rely on the "educated experts" for guidance. Decisions are made with political aims and strategies in mind and not based on an accurate understanding of the individual needs of those living homeless. The designers of the 1996 Welfare Law were naïve in believing that individual states would use their decision-making discretion morally appropriately supporting the intent of the law. The law intended to use the funds directly to help homeless people. This has not happened because federal bureaucrats are themselves removed ideologically from the state bureaucratic system that is removed from local agencies dispersing entitlements. Finally, the welfare agency personnel pull away from the person living homeless believing him/her to be unable or unwilling to do anything to change his life. The welfare system no longer *intuitively* understands the homeless person in welfare encounters.

The welfare system is separated from the lifeworld of the person living homeless and this separation reflects the growing distance between societal institutions and the individual. These institutions become dependent on legitimate orders and formal procedures needed to justify social norms. Habermas suggests that what promotes this uncoupling of the system from the lifeworld is *when action that is oriented toward success is uncoupled from action-oriented toward understanding.* This describes what has happened in social service agencies where it is assumed that homeless people are alike in that they cannot be trained to keep a job.

This system denies homeless individuals the "right" to make their own decisions (if they can) by using power and money in place of interpersonal communication. It allows those with power to tell the other how to achieve simple success without first basing this directive on what is considered normative in the community. Again, the question, *what is moral*, enters our discussion.

Habermas suggests that these systems will not become integrated until those in power can reach moral decisions from a post-conventional level of moral development. At this level of morality, institutions must do what is right because it is right and not because they are forced to do so. Without the ability to function at this higher level of morality, the social politics driving the economy will be steered through the medium of money.

THINK LIKE YOUR DISCIPLINE...Critical thinking. #5
Critical thinking involves deeply analyzing a subject from the chapter. Learn to read critically. Develop some assumptions and question them. Then evaluate your position. By considering and responding to opposing viewpoints, you strengthen your understanding. You may ask each other's assumptions but don't use the same subject from the chapter. Use a class period to listen to other viewpoints.

CHAPTER TWELVE

Immanuel Kant "We have a duty to act morally."

To be moral is first to cultivate our conscience. Kant debated that we should not be completely indifferent to others or use others for our benefit. We have moral obligations to others whether we want to or not. These obligations, to be moral, do not belong in the public domain to be enacted into law and enforced with punitive incentives. Welfare programs were considered by Kant to be institutionalized (in a formal sense) beneficence (as Kant used it means promoting the well-being of others) which promotes a paternalistic lack of respect for others. This lack of respect is played out through the treatment of them as children and the assumption that they are unable to take responsibility for their own lives and welfare. When society treats others as children encouraging dependence, this creates a society of those who are independent and those who are not.

Because we are moral-physical beings with our own constant needs, we owe others our concern and care. We must adopt others ends as our own and this requires reciprocity. It is our duty, and it is required if we are to be moral. Benhabib suggested that all should have a voice in the economic and political decisions defining their lives. Kantian arguments are used by Benhabib. She suggests from the moral point of view individuals reach a stage of reasoning where they begin to question the social validity of norms and normative institutional arrangements from the standpoint of standards of justice, fairness and impartiality.

Moral norms of conduct extend to public laws that are based on facts and the special nature of human beings and their circumstances. When the laws in the public realm disregard the dignity and rights of others, those laws are not moral. While some theorists have suggested that an ethic of care is a necessary base for an ethic of justice, *I argue* that universal principles must exist as the scaffolding on which the practice of care rests. That is, the moral principles of Kant must be assimilated into the public practice of care and these principles must accompany the practical application of welfare entitlements.

Welfare providers must recognize their profound responsibility to provide others with their concern and care. This care is, however, beneficence (beneficence is understood as the moral duty to do good for others, especially in healthcare settings) based on will and not on feelings. We must adopt others ends as our own and this requires reciprocity. It is our duty, and it is required if we are to be moral. Kant suggested, we must bring all our capacities and inclinations under the rule of reason. Reason requires that our first duty to ourselves is the cultivation of our conscience. We have a conscience whether we want one or not and in order to promote our own autonomy we have a duty not to use others as a means to an end or be indifferent to them. As members of the same community of man we owe people who live marginalized and disenfranchised lives within our affluent society our attention to their distress. As Kant suggests, this duty and obligation begs our active benevolence through the adoption of the others ends as our own. As citizens in a just society, we are allowed to act benevolently toward ourselves only on the condition that we act equally benevolently toward others (Kant, 1800/1996).

Habermas (1993) posits that repeated moral acts of care are driven by the willingness to help facilitate the good life for others. If we do not have a duty and an obligation to choose what is good for others, Habermas asks why should we be moral at all? Through the power of good reasons, that which can be articulated as collectively producing "the good life" is more than material, it is our need for dignity and respect as a person of value.

Finally, for a public policy to be moral it must be in the social interest. Any course of action is good if those who are affected by it agree that it is good. If public law forces someone to do something involuntarily, we cannot say it is in their social interest. The system coercing may benefit a lot and the person who was coerced may benefit also. However, no one may legitimately simply impose his preferences upon anyone else. For many the welfare state is visible proof that man is a moral being with a compassionate soul. For others, the welfare state is the means to moral ends creating problems for the recipients and debilitating individual initiative.

TO SUMMARIZE...

We have evaluated these public policies in terms of Joan Tronto's discussion of care as a political and moral concern. Then we looked at Seyla Benhabib's discussion of justice as the center of a universal moral theory leading to the consideration of Habermas' theory of the uncoupling of system and lifeworld. All have been applied to the interviews of the five homeless people bringing up the question of what is moral?

Since the initiation of welfare, over the succeeding years, we can ask moral questions of whether the care, provided by the 1996 Welfare Law and the McKinney Act, has helped homeless people? Has it been thoroughly informed by the universal principles of an ethic of justice? Has this care been just and changed the state of homelessness over the last several years? The immediate answer must be no.

Caring for another, we will remember, is meeting the other in a face-to-face encounter where the one offering help 'position-takes' with the one needing help. This position-taking facilitates a greater understanding of the needs of the other.

The politics of offering care for others has traditionally been in the private realm of the family and is delimited through its receptivity, responsiveness, and relatedness. This has not been happening as the result of passing the 1996 Welfare Law or the McKinney Act. If it were, happening the plight of the homeless people would have been improved in the last 20 years. It has not improved as the experiences of homeless people during the COVID-19 pandemic have shown. The provision of services for the poor and those living homeless has changed little; however, whether it can be said to be more *just* depends on who you ask.

Care is a social good but what makes it *just* or not is through its distribution. If this social good were offered in a compassionate and concerned way, receiving care would have become a social good for the recipient. However, when individuals are coerced or forced to receive this social good, or when it is offered in a demeaning or denigrating way, it ceases to be a social good for the recipient.

Welfare entitlement distribution was intended as a social good; however, it can place recipients in a paternalistic relationship fostering dependency. Additionally, it has been frustrating and dignity-denying for the homeless person trying to go through the process of applying for welfare and receiving it. When distributed in this way, the person receiving it is not being cared for and it does not provide for the recipient. Only when giving care is received as a social good and it represents what all would agree to as being what is universally right for others, is it just care.

When welfare distribution hurts the people, it is designed to help; it is not moral. Unless care is *just*, it is not moral. *The McKinney Act* offered the good to homeless people but the good was very limited, it did not go far enough. The Bush proposal in March of 2002 moved this act closer to meeting more needs of people living homeless. It accomplished this by increasing the use of mainstream federal supportive services so a larger portion of HUD's funding would go to providing housing. It implemented conferences on state team building to develop action plans to improve mainstream services that are coordinated with housing. Finally, it revised the continuum of care application to focus more on *outcomes* and less on the process. It consolidated all programs to reduce the time it took for money to reach local communities. This proposal fairly addressed existing problems. However, it cannot be said that it provided *just care*.

The 1996 Welfare Law, however, made deep cuts in low-income programs over the years from 1996 to 2015. These cuts included fundamental changes in the basic program, as well as food stamps. The Supplemental Security Income (SSI) program for the elderly and the disabled poor was reduced as well as assistance to legal immigrants. The program has not been considered *just care.*

Using this same logic, if a state is withholding funds from people who are in desperate need, preferring to leave the funds in state bank accounts, growing interest, the state is participating in an *unjust* activity. Likewise, reducing the food stamp benefit from 80 cents per person per meal to 66 cents per person per meal when the recipients qualify for no other government benefit is not *just or moral and represents inadequate care.* All or most of the benefits of legal immigrants have been eliminated. Poor immigrant children and poor immigrant elderly who have become disabled since they have been in this country and can no longer work currently are being denied benefits.

This has not care that is just. *I*t certainly is not moral, but it is in this way that legislators have declared the 1996 Welfare Law a success. **It is a success built on the denial of care** to those who are needy. What the legislators are unaware of is the significant reduction of welfare recipients has occurred because individuals have been dropped from caseloads, after supposedly reporting having found a job and therefore, no longer needing government assistance. The truth is these needy individuals and families still desperately need help but are no longer entitled to the benefits. What happens to these families, children, immigrants, and elderly? Their pain and sadness increase as they come to realize they once again have no place to go but the streets.

The care that is provided through the current welfare law is neither moral nor *just.*

GOING A STEP FURTHER...

1. Exercises in Review

Reflecting on these questions will help you engage critically with the material and deepen your understanding.

    a. What is the author's main argument? Summarize in your own words.

    b. How does the author provide support for her main argument? List and explain.

    c. What is the evidence to support the authenticity of the homeless' interviews?

    d. Consider the author's intentions and the overall tone.

    e. Does the author make any assumptions?

    f. Is the author's line of reasoning logical?

    g. Does the author try to appeal to the reader's emotions?

    h. What are your thoughts and opinions about the issues raised in this book?

2. CRITICAL THINKING about homelessness

(From the disciplines of Social Work, Psychology, Sociology, and Public Health). Can you make a statement of how your discipline promotes critical thinking?

Part I **THINK LIKE YOUR DISCIPLINE**...Critical thinking.

Critical thinking involves deeply analyzing a subject from the chapter. Learn to read critically. Develop some assumptions and question them. Then evaluate your position. By considering and responding to opposing viewpoints, you strengthen your understanding. You may ask each other's assumptions but don't use the same subject from the chapter. Use a class period to listen to each other's viewpoints.

(a) Social Work: Practical strategies to support and advocate for the homeless, human social behavior, personality, psychological disorders, and treatment. Thinking like a social worker is a way of approaching life with empathy, compassion and commitment to positive change. If your discipline is social work and part (a) is a needs assessment., same questions reply but use the constructs of that discipline?

(b) Psychology: Psychological impact of homelessness on individuals and communities. Thinking like a psychologist means being curious about why people do what they do, and underlying motives and influences are explored. Among many other concerns pathology identifies illness that appear to be chronic.

(c) Sociology: Thinking like a sociologist means you study and analyze human social behavior and the intricate relationships that shape the way people interact with each other. They collect data from research designs and their work helps shed light on complex social issues.

(d) Public Health: Social Politics and Welfare, health systems, mental health, epidemiology, infectious diseases. Thinking like a public health student involves adopting a mindset that focuses on the health and wellbeing of populations.

REFERENCES

Abell, E. & Gecas, V. (1997). "Guilt, Shame, and Family Socialization." Journal of Family Issues 18(2): 99-124.

Adler. W/ (1991). Addressing Homelessness: Status of Programs Under the Stewart B. McKinney Act and Related Legislation. Washington, D. C., National Coalition for the Homeless.

Alverson, H. et al. (1998). "Social Correlates of Competitive Employment Among People with Severe Mental Illness." Psychiatric Rehabilitation Journal 22(1): 34-40.

Anderson, L., Snow. D., & Cress, D. (1994). "Information in the Public Realm: Stigma Management and collective Action Among the Homeless." Research In Community Sociology Supplement 1: 121-143.

Anderson, L., et al. (1995). An Evaluation of State and Local Efforts to Serve the Education Needs of Homeless Children and Youth. Washington, D. C., U.S. Department of Education.

Aquino, K., & Steisel, V. (1992), "The Effects of Resource Distribution, Voice, and Decision-Framing on the Provision of Public Goods." Journal of Conflict Resolution 36(4): 665-688.

Aronson, E. (1992). The Social Animal. San Francisco, CA, Freeman.

Asher, E. (2000). Homeless Retreat. Houston, Texas, Houston chronicle: 17A.

Baier, A. C., Ed. (1987). The Need for More than Justice. Science, Morality and Feminist Theory. Calgary, The University of Calgary press.

Baxter, E. & Hopper, K. (1981). Private Lives, Public Spaces: Homeless Adults on the Streets of New York City, New York, Community Service Society.

Beatty, C. & Haggard, L. (1998). Legal Remedies to Address Discrimination Against People Who are Homeless and Have Mental Illnesses. Rockville, MD, Substance Abuse and Mental Health Services, Center for Mental Health Services, Homeless Programs Branch: whole study.

Becker, D., & Drake, R. (1993). A Working Life: The Individual Placement and support (IPS) Program. Concord, NH: New Hampshire, Dartmouth Psychiatric Research Center.

Bendor, C. (1998). Advocates Work to Combat NIMBY Program. Washington, D. C., National Law Center.

Benhabib, S. (1992). Situating the Self. New York, Routledge.

Bersoff, D. M. (1999). "Explaining Unethical Behavior Among People Motivated to Act Prosocially." Journal of Moral Education 28(4): 413-429.

Bielefeld, W. & Corbin, J. J. (1996). "The Institutionalization of Nonprofit Human Service Delivery: The Role of Political Culture." Administration & Society 28(3): 362-390.

Blum, L. (1994). Moral Perception and Particularity. Cambridge, University Press.

Bogard, C. J. (2000). "Crossing the Border: Encounters Between Homeless People and outreach Workers." Qualitative Sociology 23(3, Fall): 367-369.

Bond, G., Becket, D., Drake, R., & Vogler, K. (1997). "A Fidelity Scale for Individual Placement and Support." Rehabilitation Counseling Bulletin 40: 265-284.

Boydell, K. & Goering, P. (2000). "Narratives of Identity: Representation of Self in People who are Homeless." Qualitative Health Research 10(1): 26-39.

Burch, H. (1991). The Why's of Social Policy: Perspective on Policy Preferences. New York, Praeger.

Burt, M. (1989) Over the Edge: The Growth of Homelessness in the 1980's. New York, Russell Sage Foundation.

Burt, M. & Cohen, B. (1989) America's Homeless: Numbers, Characteristics, and Programs that Service Them. Washington, D. C., The Urban Institute.

Camus, A. (1948). The Plague. France. Librairie Galliimard.National Law Center (2001). Homelessness and Poverty: Solutions to Homelessness in America: http://www.nlchp.org/solution.htm.

National Law Center (2001). Homelessness and Poverty: Housing Options: http://www.nlchp.org/housing.htm.

Chrisman, J. M. (2000). "The Evolution of Moral Values." Humanist 60(4): 24-28.

Clarke, W.V. (1999). "The Problem of Labeling: The Semantics of Behavior." A Review of General Semantics 55(4): 404-416.

Cohen, C., Teresi, J., Holmes, D., & Roth, E. "Survival Strategies of Older Homeless Men." The Gerontologist 28(1 February): 58-65.

Cook, M. (1997). "Authenticity and Autonomy: Taylor, Habermas, and the Politics of Recognition." Political Theory 25(2): 258-288.

Copeland, V. & Wexler, S. (1985). "Policy Implementation in Social Welfare: A Framework of Analysis." Journal of Sociology and Social Welfare 12(3): 51-68.

Crane, M. (1998). "The Associations Between Mental Illness and Homelessness Among Older People: An Exploratory Study." Aging and Mental Health 2(3 August):171-180.

Crane M. & Warnes, A. (2000). "Evictions and Prolonged Homelessness." Housing Studies 15(5): 757-772.

Culyer, A. (1973). The Economics of Social Policy. Cambridge, MA, Dunellen.

de Beauvoir, Simone (1953). The Second Sex. Trans. and Ed. H. M. Pashley, New York, Knopf.

Dolgoff, R., & Feldstein, D. (2000). Understanding Social Welfare. Needham Heights, MA, Allyn and Bacon.

Donnelly, D., Cook, K., & Wilson, L. (1999). "Provision and Exclusion: The Dual Face of Services to Battered Women in Three Deep South States." Violence-Against-Women 5(7 July): 710-741.

Drake, R., Osher, F., & Wallach, M. (1991). "Homelessness and Dual Diagnosis." American Psychologist 44(1): 1149-1158.

Everingham, C. (2001). "Reconstituting Community: Social Justice, Social Order, and the Politics of Community." Australian Journal of Social Issues 36(2): 105-117

Fellin, P. (1998). "Development of Capital in Poor, Inner-City Neighborhoods." Journal of Community Practice **5**(3): 87-98.

Fischer, C. (1984). The Urban Experience. Boston, MA, Harcourt, Brace, and Jovanovich.

Foscarinas, M. (1996). The Federal Response: The Steward B. McKinney Homeless Assistance Act. Homelessness in America. National Coalition for the Homeless. Washington, D. C.

Foxall, G., & Greenley, G. (1998). "The Affective Structure of Consumer Situations. Environment and Behavior **30**(6): 781-798.

France, A-C, & Alpher., V. (1995). "Structural Analysis of Social Behavior and

Perceptions of Caregiving." Journal of Psychology **129**(4) 375-389.

Fuchs, E., & McAllister, W. (1996). "The Continuum of Care: A Report on the New

Federal Policy to Address Homelessness." Community Connections **32**:34-95.

Gaiman, H. (1996). Neverwhere. New York, Avon.

Geremek, B. (1994). Poverty: A History. Oxford, UK, Blackwell.

Giddens, A. (1979). Central Problems in Social Theory: Action, Structure and

Contradiction in Social Analysis. University of California, Berkeley.

Gilliatt, S., & Fenwick, J. (2000). "Public Services and the Consumer: Empowerment or Control?" Social Policy & Administration **34**(3): 333-350.

Gilligan, C. (1987). Moral Orientation and Moral Development, Rowman and Littlefield, New York.

Glasser, N. (1998). Giving Voice to Homeless People in Policy, Practice and

Research. National Symposium on Homelessness Research, Washington, D. C., Department of Health and Human Services.

Goffman, I. (1963). <u>Stigma: Notes on the Management of Spoiled Identity</u>. New York, Simon and Schuster.

Golden, S. (2000). <u>The Women Outside: Meanings and Myths of Homelessness</u>. Berkeley, CA, University of California Press.

Goodman, D. (2000). "Motivating People from Privileged Groups to Support Social Justice." <u>Teachers College Record</u> **102**(3): 1061-1086.

Greenberg, M., Levin-Epstein, J., Hutson, R., Ooms, T., Schumacher, R., Turetsky, V., & Engstrom, D. (2000). Welfare Reauthorization: An early Guide to the Issues. Washington, D. C., Center for Law and Social Policy.

Gudzowsky, N. (2002). Peter Edelman: Policy Work with a Cause. Washington, D. C. Horizon Poverty Series: people, places, and solutions: whole article.

Gullati, P. (1995). "Ideology, Public Policy and Homeless Families." <u>Journal of Sociology and Social Welfare</u> **35**(1): 113-127.

Guttmann, A., & Thompson, D. (1990). "Moral Conflict and Political Consensus." <u>Ethics</u>: 64-88.

Habermas, J. (1973). <u>Legitimation Crisis</u>. Boston, MA, Beacon Press.

Habermas, J. (1984). <u>The Theory of Communicative Action: Reason and the Rationalization of Society</u>. Boston, MA, The MIT Press.

Habermas, J. (1987). <u>The Theory of Communicative Action: Lifeworld and System: A critique of functionalist reason</u>. Boston, MA, The MIT Press.

Habermas, J. (1993). <u>Justification and Application: Remarks on Discourse Ethics.</u>Cambridge, MA, The MIT Press.

Halliday, S. (2000). "Institutional Racism in Bureaucratic Decision-Making: A Case Study in the Administration of Homelessness Law." <u>Journal of Law and Society</u> **27**(3): 449-472.

Halter, A. (1995). "Homeless in Philadelphia: A Qualitative Study of the Impact of State Welfare Reform on Individuals. " <u>Journal of Sociology and Social Welfare</u> **35**(1):64-72.

Harden, G. (1968). "The Tragedy of the Commons." <u>Science</u> **162**: 1243-1248.

Held, V. (1995). Justice and Care: Essential Readings in Feminist Ethics. Boulder, CO, Westview Press.

Hemming, J. (1996). "Morality After Myth." Journal of Moral Education 25(1): 39-46.

National Coalition of the Homeless (1999). The Steward B. McKinney Homeless Assistance Act. Washington, D. C.: whole report.

National Alliance to End Homelessness (2000). A Status Report on Hunger and Homelessness in American Cities, U. S. Conference of Mayors.

Hudson, C. (1998). An Interdependency Model of Homelessness. The Dynamics of Social Disintegration. Lapeter, Cerredigion, Wales, The Edwin Mellen Press, Ltd.

Jenks, C. (1991). Rethinking Social Policy: Race, Poverty and the Underclass. New York, Harper, Collins Publishers, Inc.

Johnson, J. (1991). "Habermas on Strategic and Communicative Action." Political Theory 19(2): 181-201.

Johnson, R. (1999): "Internal Reasons and the Conditional Fallacy." Philosophical Quarterly 49(4): 53-72.

Kant, I. (1800). The Metaphysics of Morals. Cambridge, MA, Cambridge University.

Koegel, P., Sullivan, G., Jinnett, K., Morton, S., Jackson, C., & Miu, A. (2000).

Characterizing the Homeless Population in Houston. Washington, D. C., National Institutes of Mental Health. RO1 MH 50632

Koggel, C. (2001). Care and Justice Rexamined and Revised, 20th WCP, 2002.

Korth, B. (1998). "A Reformation of Care as a Pragmatic Concept: A Qualitative Study of An Adult Friendship Group." Unpublished Doctor of Philosophy Dissertation, University of Houston, May, 1998.

Kozol, J. (1988). Rachel and her children: Homeless families in America. New York, Fawcett Columbine.

Kroeger-Mappes, J. (1994). "The Ethic of Care vis-vis the Ethic of Rights: A Problem for Contemporary Moral Theory." Hypatia 9(3): 108-131.

Kulza, Jl, & Keigher, S. (1991). "The Elderly "New Homeless: An Emerging Population at Risk." Social Work 36(4 July): 288-293.

Law, S. & Kong, C. (1999). "The Acceptance of Lonely Others: Effects of Loneliness and Gender of the Target Person and Loneliness of the Perceiver."Journal of Social Psychology 139(2): 229-242.

Levy, S. (1999). "Reducing Prejudice: Lessons From Social-Cognitive Underlying Perceiver Differences in Prejudice." Journal of Social Issues **Winter**: www.findarticle.com.

Lewin, R. (1996). Compassion. Northvale, H. J., Jason Aronson, Inc.

Mason, J. (2002). "Welfare up for further tinkering: Bush's plan facing hurdle in Congress." The Houston Chronicle, April 9:10A.

Lingis, A. (1994). The Community of Those Who Have Nothing in Common. Bloomington, IL, Indiana University Press.

Luhrmann, T. (2000). Of Two Minds. New York, Alfred A. Knopf.

Marwell, G., & Ames, R. (1979). "Experiments on the Provision of Public Good 1: Resources, Interest Group Size, and the Free-Rider Problem." American Journal of Sociology 84: 1335-1360.

Marx, K. (1971). Economy, Class, and Social Revolution. New York, Scribner & Sons.

Maybach, C. (1996). "Investing in Urban Community Needs." Education & Urban Society 28(2): 224-237.

McClain, P. (1995). "Thirty Years of Urban Policies." Urban Affairs Review 30(4): 641-645.

McLaren, P. (1992). "Collisions with Otherness." International Journal of Qualitative Studies in Education 5(1): 77-92.

Mead, G. H. (1934). Mind, Self & Society: From the Standpoint of a Social Behaviorist. Chicago, IL, The University of Chicago Press.

Meade, L. (1986). Beyond Entitlement: The Social Obligations of Citizenship. New York, Free Press.

Mellinger, J. (1989). "Emergency Housing for Frail Older Adults." The Gerontologist **29**(3 June): 401-404.

Miller, C. (2001). "A Theoretical Perspective on Coping With Stigma." Journal of Social Issues **Spring**(www.findarticles.com).

Miller, D. (2000). Principles of Social Justice. Cambridge, MA, Harvard University Press.

Miller, S. (1993). "The Politics of Respect." Social Policy **23**(3): 44-52.

Moynihan, D. (1993). "Toward a New Intolerance." Public Interest **112**(Summer): 119-123.

Murphy, T. (1994). "Discourse Ethics: Moral Theory or Political Ethic." New German Critique **66**:111-136.

Murphy, T. (1994). "Discourse Ethics & Civil Society." New German Critique **66**: 36-52.

National Coalition for the Homeless Fact Sheet. #18 (1999). The McKinney Act. Washington, D. C., National Coalition for the Homeless.

National Law Center on Homelessness and poverty (2001) Civil Rights Violations. Washington, D. C.

Noddings, N. (1984) Caring: A Feminine Approach to Ethics and Moral Education. Berkeley, The Regents of the University of California.

Nussbaum, V. (2000). Women and Human Development: The Capabilities Approach. Cape Town, South Africa, Cambridge University Press.

Oyserman, D. (2001) "Stigma: An Insider's View." Journal of Social Issues Spring: www.findarticles.com.

Peressini, T. (1999). Homeless Older Adults in Canada. Society for the Study of Social Problems.

Council of Homeless Persons (1999). "Elderly Homeless People." Family Matters **52** (Autumn): 40-41.

Phelan, J., Link, B., Moore, R., & Stueve, A. (1997). "The Stigmas of Homelessness: The Impact of the Label Homeless on Attitudes Toward Poor Persons." Social Psychology Quarterly **60**(4): 323-337.

Pickford, D. (2002)."New National Survey of the Nation's Poor Challenges Success of Welfare Reform." Press Release. National Homeless Organization, April 19.

Primus, W. & Daugirdas, K. (2000). Program Funds Services for Vulnerable Low-Income Children and People Who are Elderly or Disabled. Washington, D. C., Center on Budget and Policy Priorities.

Quimby, E. (1995). "Homeless Clients' Perspectives on Recovery in the Washington, D. C. Dual Diagnosis Project." Contemporary Drug Problems **22**(2): 265-269.

Quimby, E., Drake, R., & Becker, D. (2001). Ethnographic Findings from the Washington, D. C. Vocational Services Study." Psychiatric Rehabilitation Journal 24(4): 368-375.

Rank, M. (1995). "A View from the Inside Out: Recipients' Perceptions of Welfare." Journal of Sociology and Social Welfare **34**(1): 27-47.

Rapoport, A. (1988). "Provision o f Step-Level Public Goods: Effects of Inequality in Resources." Journal of Personality and Social Psychology **54**(3): 432-440.

Rawls, J. (2001). Justice As Fairness: A restatement. Cambridge, MA, The Belknap Press of Harvard University Press.

Reitz-Pustejovsky, Marilyn (2002). Is the Care We Provide the Homeless Just? The Ethic of Justice Informing the Ethic of Care. The Journal of Social Distress and the Homeless, Vol. 11, No. 3, July 2002

Rog, D., & Hollupka, C. (1998). Reconnecting Homeless Individuals and Families to the Community, Washington, D. C., National SymposiumHomelessness Research.

Sampson, E. (1977). "Psychology and the American Ideal." Journal of Personality and Social Psychology **35**: 767-782.

Sampson, E. (1988). "The Debate on Individualism: Indigenous Psychologies of the Iundividual and Their Role in Personal and Societal Function." American Psychologist **43**: 15-22.

Sard, B. (2001). Using TANF Funds for Housing-Related Benefits to prevent Homelessness. Washington, D. C., Center on Budget and Policy Priorities.

Savner, S., Strawn, J., & Greeberg, M. (2002). TANF Reauthorization: Opportunities to Reduce Poverty by Improving Employment Outcomes. Washington, D. C., CLASP: whole report.

Sexton, P. (1983). "The Life of the Homeless." Dissent **30**(1): 79-84.

Sheer, V., & Weigold, M. (1995). "Managing Threats to Identity: The Accountability Triangle and Strategic Accounting." Communication Research **22**(4): 592-612.

National Coalition for the Homeless Sheet #15. (1999). Homelessness Among Elderly Persons, June. www.nch.ari.net/elderly

Snow, D., & Anderson, L. (1993). Down on Their Luck: A Study of Homeless Street People. Berkeley, CA, University of California Press.

Soss, J. (1999). "Welfare Application Encounters." Administration and Society **31**(1): 50-95.

Spanos, N. (1994). "Multiple Identity Enactments and Multiple Personality Disorder: A Socio-cognitive Perspective." Psychological Bulletin **116**: 143-165.

Spence, J. (1985). "Achievement American Style: The Rewards and Costs of Individualism." American Psychologist **40**: 1285-1295.

Sullivan, J. (1992). "A Family Systems-Oriented Approach to the Treatment of the Homeless, Mentally Ill, Older Women." Dissertation Abstracts international. The Humanities and Scial Sciences **52**(9): March, 3434-A.

Sullivan, J., Koegel, P., Morton, S., Jackson, C., & Miu, A. (2000). Public Sector Service Use and the Homeless Mentally Ill, National Institute of Mental Health.

Super, D., Parrott, S., Steinmetz, S., & Mann, C. (1996): The New Welfare Law – Summary, Center on Budget and Policy Priorities. **2002.**

Taylor, C. (1979). <u>Hegel and Modern Society</u>. Cambridge, U.K., Cambridge University Press.

Tjeltveit, A. (2001). "Natural Moral Sense as Basis for Professional Ethics: An Important Proposal But Unlikely to Produce Excellence." <u>Journal of Psychology and Theology</u> **29**(3): 235-239.

Tracey, E., & Stoecker, R. (1995). "Homelessness: The Service Providers' Perspective on Blaming the Victim." <u>Journal of Sociology and Social Welfare</u> **30**(1): 43-59.

Tronto, J. (1991). "Reflections on Gender, Morality, and Power: Caring and the Moral Problem of Otherness." Unpublished Paper. Hunter College of the City University of New York, March.

Tronto, J. (1994). <u>Moral Boundaries</u>. New York, Routledge.

Tully, C., & Jacobson, S. (1994). "The homeless Elderly: America's Forgotten Populations." <u>Journal of Gerontological Social Work</u> **22**(3/4): 61-81.

Van Knippenberg, D. (2000). "Work Motivation and Performance: A Social Identity Perspective." <u>Applied Psychology</u> **49**(3): 357-352.

Vance, D. (1995). "A Portrait of Older Homeless Mens' Identifying Hopelessness & Adaptation." <u>Journal of Social Distress and the Homeless</u> **4**(1 January):57-71.

Walker, M. (1998). <u>Moral Understandings: A Feminist Study in Ethics</u>. New York, Routledge.

Wilensky, H. & Lebeaux, C. (1965). Industrial Society and Social Welfare. New York, Free Press.

Williams, M. (1995). "Justice Toward Groups: Political not Juridical." <u>Political Theory</u> **23**(1): 67-91.

Willis, P. (1977). <u>Learning to Labor</u>. Lexington, MA, Health.

The Tragedy of Homelessness

Immanuel Kant posited that we have moral obligations to others whether we want to or not. The moral act of caring involves care accomplished in real situations with real people. It is caring that is delimited by moral virtues of receptivity, responsiveness, and relatedness. Given these virtues one is charged with acting fairly.

According to Kant, our first duty is the cultivation of our own conscience. This duty exists as an *a priori* obligation that charges active benevolence through the adoption of another's ends as our own.

The tragedy of homelessness is that needy families still desperately need help. Failure to respond because we choose to ignore another's reality as a possibility of our own, represents our deficits as a person, a person denuded of morality.

www.ingramcontent.com/pod-product-compliance
Ingram Content Group UK Ltd.
Pitfield, Milton Keynes, MK11 3LW, UK
UKHW020906140225
454953UK00021B/121

9 798822 968684